PLAYS FOR PERFORMANCE

A series designed for
contemporary production and study
Edited by
Nicholas Rudall and Bernard Sahlins

CARLO GOLDONI

The Servant of
Two Masters

In a New Adaptation by
Dorothy Louise

Ivan R. Dee
CHICAGO

Library of Congress Cataloging-in-Publication Data:
Louise, Dorothy.
    The Servant of two masters / Carlo Goldoni ; in a new adaptation by Dorothy Louise.
        p. cm. — (Plays for performance)
    ISBN 1-56663-536-5 (alk. paper)
    1. Master and servant—Drama. 2. Domestics—Drama.
I. Goldoni, Carlo, 1707–1793. Servitore di due padroni.
II. Title. III. Series.

PS3612.O8S47 2003
812'.6—dc21   2003043982

INTRODUCTION
by Dorothy Louise

Directing *The Servant of Two Masters* a few years ago at Franklin and Marshall College became an unusually pleasurable experience, largely because we began with an earlier draft of this adaptation, tailored particularly to the interests and abilities of young actors.

Over the course of rehearsals, the working script shifted and developed as the actors grew in confidence and familiarity with their roles. Our experience bore out the wisdom of the Italian popular tradition of strong character types, as clearly stamped as the masked characters from whom they descend, and each obsessed with a purpose. In addition to several pairs of lovers, the play features servants who outsmart their masters by combining guile with good luck, fathers whose greed takes precedence over their children's affections, and children whose desires to marry for love eventually prevail over their fathers' more mundane, middle-class obsessions with propriety and property. These stereotypes also happen to be part of young actors' experience: they have recently, or are currently, struggling with parental proscriptions, budding infatuations, full-blown passions, and apparently arbitrary rules and regulations. So they attack these situations with robust appetites.

We also availed ourselves of a second critical ingredient of the commedia tradition, improvisation, find-

3

ing in familiar situations many opportunities for contemporary riffs on current gossip and international crises. The particulars may fade, but the categories remain, and future productions ought to take advantage of them. The poor are not alone in being always with us: as staples of our social scene we can also rely upon corrupt politicians, celebrities who live to be seen and misquoted in the tabloids, and CEOs whose signing bonuses and stock options can never include too many zeros. So one may wish to substitute a more recent reference for Michael and Lisa Marie, President Reagan, Ivan Boesky, or Whitewater, and a large part of the delight of working on this play will consist in exploring the particulars and inserting the embellishments that result.

One final point about actors. Many classics require more men than women for the company, yet many small theatres have far more women than men interested in acting. So one is always looking for scripts that answer this need and address this imbalance without unduly distorting the work itself. Brighella, traditionally a male, is here cast as a woman, and even serves the fun more roguishly by colluding with Beatrice, who, one woman to another, confides the truth behind her male disguise. Sisterhood can indeed generate power. Further, Goldoni's two male servants who assist Truffaldino in his whirlwind *tour de force* appearances as dual versions of himself are reborn here as Nora and Pandora, displaying the same pettiness and frustration that characterize their antecedents. In fact a feminist sensibility infuses various moments, ranging from Beatrice's daring resourcefulness to Smeraldina's sassy prologue, an item wholly invented for this adaptation.

In commedia, the actors are nearly everything. And yet in all theatrical forms, of course, the architecture and clothing that scenic and costume design-

4

ers provide make up a good part of the rest. Although any production may carry the contemporary reference into costume and setting, we found that an amalgam of Venetian inn and street scene of the mid-eighteenth century suited our purpose, providing more attractive challenges for the designers and a fresher experience for the actors. As usual, they found that in some important sense the habit does indeed make the monk, whether this was Truffaldino's floppy hat secured on one side with a rabbit's foot, or Brighella's fanciful toque printed in peppers and pomegranates, or Dr. Lombardi's voluminous, billowing academic gown, its metallic threads swirling paisley. A bit fantastic, perhaps, and yet appropriate to this fabulous comic world of unbridled invention.

The street scene lends itself to appropriate athleticism, especially in the essential scene where Truffaldino must serve both masters at the same time. In our production we multiplied the physical obstacles by staging Beatrice's dinner upstairs right of center, and Florindo's dinner symmetrically opposite. Thus Truffaldino sprinted from one second-story to another via the ground level, where Nora and Pandora handed off the required courses, and where he might also have a split second alone to savor the odd meatball or to ascertain the sweetness of Brighella's peaches (another joke possible only if she is female). Upstage center, a fanciful version of the Bridge of Sighs provided a perilous platform upon which Lombardi and Pantalone could confront each other, adding to the compositional variety of the stage picture and lending a thrill when the fathers risked a fall.

Despite the many snares strewn along their paths, the lovers and servants tiptoe, slalom, and sometimes just take the leap of faith, occasionally getting snagged, sometimes caught fast, but finally bursting free into the open landscape of a harmonious future, in which lovers are fittingly matched, fathers are appropriately cajoled and mollified, and servants and masters will presumably live in a new social order that resolves the chaos of their journey. The play provides pure joy. Goldoni's comic world may flirt with death, but verified reports of dying prove false, and suicidal urges short-lived. We land resoundingly on the side of life.

CHARACTERS

SMERALDINA, maid to Clarice
FLORINDO, in love with Beatrice
BEATRICE, in love with Florindo
SILVIO, in love with Clarice
PANTALONE, father of Clarice
CLARICE, in love with Silvio
DR. LOMBARDI, father of Silvio
BRIGHELLA, innkeeper (a woman in this version)
TRUFFALDINO, servant to Beatrice, then to Florindo
PORTER
PANDORA and NORA, servants at Brighella's inn

The Servant of Two Masters

PROLOGUE

Venice in about 1780, variously the street and the inn.

SMERALDINA: Ladies and Gentlemen, but most
   especially
The unsung ladies, such as they be!
If not to the manner born,
Then to the manner bred!
Instructed in the lady arts
Of cooking pot, button, and bed!
Welcome to Venezia!
The jewel of Italia!
Its people all well-spoken,
Their speeches all well-said!
Our plot concerns two lovers—

FLORINDO: *(appearing at a window)* I am one . . .

BEATRICE: *(appearing on a balcony)* And I the other.

SMERALDINA: Flying from Turin to Venice, fleeing cus-
tom and convention.

FLORINDO: Oh, Beatrice—I will gallop to the ends of
the earth, if only, at last, you will be mine! I will ro-
tate repeatedly in time's winged chariot, until the
day when I can gather you to my smoldering
bosom! Gladly will I fling away power and position,
endure the clucking tongues of gossips and gad-
flys, and suffer the slings and arrows of Lombardis
and archers—if only I can finally cradle you in my
sinuous—sinewy—arms!

BEATRICE: If not here, in paradise! *(fading out)*

FLORINDO: I prefer here, but I'll settle for paradise. *(closing window)*

SMERALDINA: Prenuptials and betrothals, weddings and funerals—this play has everything! And although the weddings don't come till the end, the betrothal's right at the top! Solve that riddle. Meanwhile . . . our revels now are begun.
Naturelle, we are your servitori—
Finalmente, you are our padroni—
The world of Venezia, Italia, amore!
Of prego, and grazie, and scusi, per favore!
Permesso adesso—your indulgence now—
Amuse you, excuse you—we know we know how!

ACT 1

Scene 1

A small square in Venice. All have taken their places for the formal betrothal ceremony.

SILVIO: Here is my hand, and with it my whole heart, and with that whatever else I am and possess in all the world, without stint or exception, explicit or im-, for I am yours, yours, yours, at your disposal, lock, stock, and barrel, from this day forward. *(throws himself at Clarice's feet, nearly pulling her over)*

PANTALONE: Well! The fulsomeness of youth! *(to Clarice)* And you, my dear—speak up, speak up. The man can't have all the lines. Especially when the woman's my daughter and I am paying for the betrothal supper! Come—give him your hand. Later we can—uh—refine—the prenuptial agreement.

CLARICE: I wish I could say how I feel, but I never was very good with words. Sometimes I'm like, so articulate I'm a regular waterfall of verbal felicity. Other times, I, well, uh, I can hardly scrape up a shopworn cliché from the bottom of the barrel. Oh, dearest Silvio! *(throwing herself at him, she nearly knocks him over)* I, too, am yours forever and ever!

LOMBARDI: And so forth and so on, ad infinitum.

SILVIO: Wife!

13

CLARICE: Husband!

(they embrace fiercely, sighing and snorting)

PANTALONE: All right, all right, that's enough.

SMERALDINA: *(aside)* I know how they feel—I'm dying to get married!

LOMBARDI: Enough!

(they split)

PANTALONE: There's still a wedding to come, you know. No anti-climaxes. Gives theatre a bad name.

SILVIO: The betrothal's just as binding as the marriage.

CLARICE: We two are one from this moment on. *(singing)* You for me, dear—

SILVIO: Only two for tea, dear.

LOMBARDI: No rush, no rush. Young people forever dashing hither and yon, pillar to post, rollerblading, Internetting. . . .

SILVIO: Created to be together.

CLARICE: Made for each other.

SMERALDINA: Oooh! Aren't they just perfect?

CLARICE: Adam and Eve.

SILVIO: Abelard and Heloise.

CLARICE: Michael and Lisa Marie. No, no—Nicholas Cage and Lisa Marie. No, no—

SMERALDINA: Perfect, perfect, perfect!

PANTALONE: Let's keep a little perspective until the papers are signed.

14

LOMBARDI: I've gained a daughter! *(embracing Clarice; aside)* And a dowry!

PANTALONE: I've gained a son. *(embracing Silvio; aside)* And a shrewd financial understanding.

LOMBARDI: The witnesses, please.

BRIGHELLA: In witness thereof, I sign. *(doing so with a flourish)*

SMERALDINA: Me, too. *(ditto)*

BRIGHELLA: *(writing)* Smeraldina, her mark—there! *(a third, climactic flourish)*

LOMBARDI: *(stamping the document on each syllable)* Du-ly no-ta-rized pro bo-no! Sub spe-ci-e ae-ter-ni-ta-tis. Lux! Lex! Crux! Hex! Arrivederci, Oedipus Rex! *(business with sealing wax, seals)*

SMERALDINA: Let me see, let me see! *(scrutinizing document, unable to make anything of it)*

BRIGHELLA: *(turning it right side up)* There!

SMERALDINA: *(uncomprehending)* Ah.

LOMBARDI: Well, I hope it won't be taken amiss, or viewed as untoward, rude, even, but I'm as hungry as an honest monk after his Lenten fast.

PANTALONE: *(signaling Brighella)* A light repast awaits. *(Brighella and Smeraldina go into the inn)* Like these two lovebirds, we wouldn't want to spoil the wedding by—celebrating—too early, eh? Too grand a feast now would overshadow the coming one. I have ordered a fitting—snack.

LOMBARDI: Ah.

PANTALONE: These days, people don't appreciate a repast unless it's light, light, light. Evanescent as a

15

butterfly wing, unsubstantial as Reagan's memoirs—

LOMBARDI: Actually, I prefer substance.

PANTALONE: You think I am made of money?

LOMBARDI: Well, you're not hurting, are you?

PANTALONE: Lombardi, Lombardi! Have you checked out the cost of betrothals and weddings lately?

LOMBARDI: Admittedly, I—

PANTALONE: And why should all the burden fall upon the father of the bride?

LOMBARDI: Nothing too good for the bride. Who knows that better than her father?

PANTALONE: The last thing a bridegroom needs is a bride grown accustomed to extravagance. A good wife is a frugal wife!

LOMBARDI: Oh, it's fine, fine, please, you never know when to quit.

PANTALONE: Everything these days is light, refined, above the vulgar rough-and-tumble, on the side of the angels, eh Clarice?

CLARICE: What's that, Father?

PANTALONE: A marriage made in heaven. No need for food in paradise.

LOMBARDI: Who's in paradise?

SILVIO: I am, Father.

CLARICE: And I.

PANTALONE: You see? All for the best.

CLARICE: Fate.

SILVIO: Destiny.

PANTALONE: Amazing how time heals all wounds, as the ancients say.

SILVIO: I shall compare thee to a summer's day.

CLARICE: Hot, hot.

SILVIO: Humid, humid.

PANTALONE: I was—how shall I put it?—simply shattered! In shards! *(to audience)* Clarice promised to Federigo Rasponi, and he, suddenly dead! Cut down in a duel! Something about his sister! Oh, calamity! Disaster! Armageddon! All those financial—I mean, familial—arrangements, poof! Like that! Gone for naught! Written on the wind, witnessed on the water!

CLARICE: *(moaning)* Dying of thirst.

SILVIO: *(moaning)* About to expire.

PANTALONE: And then—this! *(slaps Silvio on the back)*

(Brighella enters with a tray of glasses of champagne, and serves them around. Smeraldina follows with a platter of microscopic canapés. Lombardi puts on his glasses and scrutinizes the tray.)

SILVIO: *(snapping to)* His gross misfortune, my great good luck! I only hope you, Clarice, feel the same!

CLARICE: Are you really asking?

SILVIO: I like to hear you say it. I love to hear you say it. Oh, divine lady, say it, say it, say it!

CLARICE: I am a paragon of virtue, a dutiful daughter. But my heart has always belonged to you. You are in my daily orifices—I mean, orisons—prayers!

17

Give us this day our daily bed. And now, it's official!

PANTALONE: A toast!

LOMBARDI: *(to himself)* Toast? *(frantically looking)* Where?

PANTALONE: And after our toast?

LOMBARDI: Jam! Cheese! Twinkies! Gatorade!

BRIGHELLA: A light collation awaits within.

PANTALONE: To the betrothed, my daughter and almost son-in-law!

LOMBARDI: To the future joining of our families, blending the best of commerce *(with a nod to Pantalone)* with the best that learning has to offer!

(all drink as Truffaldino rushes in)

TRUFFALDINO: Ladies and gentlemen! If I may be so bold!

SMERALDINA: Ooh! Isn't he the one!

PANTALONE: Sir, this is a private party.

TRUFFALDINO: I thought it was a public street.

LOMBARDI: We are about to go in, but he is right, in point of law this is a public thoroughfare, and he has as much right, jus vulgar est universalis semper, or, in the vernacular, the common law always applies. Even in those cases where the fellow has a questionable accent and appears to be a cheat and a scoundrel.

TRUFFALDINO: Signor Pantalone?

PANTALONE: I haven't had the pleasure.

TRUFFALDINO: Say no more, sir, I am at your service.

PANTALONE: To the point, to the point, our supper awaits.

TRUFFALDINO: Our supper? Why, thank you. I am often hungry, usually starving. But today I am utterly famished. *(to audience)* I've heard Venetians are rough, but these people are really considerate! *(starting in)*

PANTALONE: *(cutting him off)* Your business?

TRUFFALDINO: *(making a U-turn)* Business, business, yes. I represent my master, who desires to pay his respects to Signor Pantalone—that is to say, you sir.

PANTALONE: I know that, I know, get on with it, who is your master?

TRUFFALDINO: Signor Federigo Rasponi! *(supplying tuckets and sennets)* Illustrissimo! Bellissimo! Etceterissimo!

(all gasp, freeze)

PANTALONE: *(to audience)* The dead Federigo? Betrothed of Clarice? *(to Truffaldino)* Who?

LOMBARDI: Who?

CLARICE: *(about to faint)* Who?

TRUFFALDINO: *(to Smeraldina)* Even though I'm not from Venice, you understand me, don't you? I mean, am I speaking Greek or what? All I said was, my master is—

SMERALDINA: Your master doesn't concern me. You, on the other hand . . .

TRUFFALDINO: Allow me, Signorina *(with a sweeping bow)*, to present myself: Truffaldin' Battocchio from Bergamo!

SMERALDINA: Oh! You sound like a poet!

TRUFFALDINO: I do, don't I? Hm! Didn't know I had it in me.

PANTALONE: Just a minute!

TRUFFALDINO: *(to Smeraldina, setting the beat)* And may I say—

SMERALDINA: In your own sweet way—

TRUFFALDINO: You're a tres beauté—

SMERALDINA: Hey, hey, hey—you've made my day!

PANTALONE: Now cut that out!

LOMBARDI: Without a doubt—

PANTALONE: Mush and nonsense!

LOMBARDI: You need a talent scout to tell you about—

PANTALONE: The ins and outs of getting some clout—

LOMBARDI: To advance your career as a roustabout—

PANTALONE: What am I saying? Stop, stop!

LOMBARDI: Who specializes in sauerkraut!

TRUFFALDINO: Now I don't know what he's talking about!

PANTALONE: Who is your master?

TRUFFALDINO: *(nearly breaking Pantalone's eardrum)* Signor Fe-de-ri-go Ra-spo-ni!

PANTALONE: Please! You must be mistaken.

TRUFFALDINO: I know my master's name, sir. Rhymes with rigatoni! Macaroni! Pantalone and riding on a pony! Do you take me for an idiot?

LOMBARDI: As a matter of fact—

PANTALONE: A madman, perhaps.

LOMBARDI: Or a dupe. We must weigh all the alternatives. Or a candidate for the insanity defense. Are you seeking asylum, my boy? Here in Venice we espouse republican principles, never fear. Whatever your state! Mens sana is all well and good, but the simplicimi are prone to naiveté, as the French say, and—

PANTALONE: Don't nitpick, whatever! Signor Federigo Rasponi is dead!

TRUFFALDINO: What?!

LOMBARDI: His soul has transmigrated, sir. Flights of angels and so forth and so on, seraphim, cherubim, thrones, and dominations!

PANTALONE: Damnation!

TRUFFALDINO: No!

BRIGHELLA: He has gone to his just reward.

(funereal chant under)

TRUFFALDINO: He has?

PANTALONE: No doubt about it.

TRUFFALDINO: I am dumbstruck!

PANTALONE: Now we're getting somewhere. Yes, yes—life is but a fleeting moment!

LOMBARDI: Ars longa, vita brevis, requiescat in pace, per omnia saecula saeculorum!

TRUFFALDINO: I left him alive at the dock! Not two minutes ago! Are you sure about this?

PANTALONE: Is a Venetian blind?

LOMBARDI: If you need a document, I can—

TRUFFALDINO: Never mind, never mind! Just when I'd finally found a decent job. Nothing lavish, just—what am I thinking? My poor master! He must have fallen into the canal! *(rushes out)*

LOMBARDI: I'm sure there's a death certificate somewhere.

SMERALDINA: Such loyalty! Such feeling!

PANTALONE: Such knavery! I guess we showed him! Now! Let us resume.

LOMBARDI: The collation awaits!

SILVIO: *(to Clarice)* Are you all right, dearest?

CLARICE: What if it were true?

SILVIO: That's the trouble with having these little gatherings in the piazza. Any loony tune can wander in.

CLARICE: Oh, Silvio! How you put things!

SILVIO: Well, thanks. And what if Rasponi were here? So what! I don't give a gnat's ear! You are mine now. Aaal mine! *(crushing her)* He is too late!

TRUFFALDINO: *(rushing in)* Oh, sirs! Shame on you! Shame, shame, shame! To take in a stranger like that! Have you no honor? It's a good thing I'm young and healthy—

SMERALDINA: You sure are. *(to herself)* I don't really care—I'm not particular!

TRUFFALDINO: Because I nearly had a heart attack!

PANTALONE: If you will excuse us, sir.

TRUFFALDINO: I will not excuse you, I will not! I may, in fact, be forced to challenge you. *(pulls his battochio [slapstick] from his belt, brandishes it)*

LOMBARDI: My good man, please—

TRUFFALDINO: Don't you "my good man" me! To pierce me to the heart like that! My master dead! What kind of people live in Venice? Mean-spirited charlatans? Cruel pranksters!? Ghoulish perverts?!

LOMBARDI: *(to Pantalone)* You were right the first time. Totally deluded! Be careful.

PANTALONE: *(humoring Truffaldino)* You perhaps have caught sight of your master just now?

TRUFFALDINO: Perhaps! Caught sight! I stared at him from head to toe!

LOMBARDI: Possibly an apparition.

TRUFFALDINO: I clasped him by the knees to verify his corporeality! I spoke to him and he answered back, though what he thought of me I'm afraid to guess! I'm in excellent health, Truffaldino, excellent! Of course! Why do you ask! Well, I said, because I'd heard a rumor that you were dead. Dead, he said, and laughed out loud. Do I look dead? Do I sound dead? And what of Signor Pantalone? May I pay my respects? *(to Pantalone)* I told him you were engaged. He asks only for a few minutes.

PANTALONE: Signor Federigo.

TRUFFALDINO: Signor Federigo.

PANTALONE: *(to Lombardi)* Stark raving—

LOMBARDI: You have proof?

TRUFFALDINO: *(to Smeraldina)* No one takes the word of a gentleman in Venice?

SMERALDINA: In Venice, servants are not regarded as gentlemen.

TRUFFALDINO: *(taking umbrage)* If I must prove it, I will prove it. *(to Smeraldina)* And later, we will resume our acquaintanceship.

(Leaves. After a moment, Smeraldina follows.)

CLARICE: Oh, Silvio, I'm all a-tremble!

SILVIO: Be still, my love. Your Silvio is here. Lean on him, as the clinging ivy curls about the oak.

CLARICE: Oh, Silvio!

SILVIO: Besides, as I told you, he's too late! Right, Father?

LOMBARDI: I await the evidence, quod erit demonstrandum, that is to say, it remains to be seen.

PANTALONE: An impostor, no doubt. A punk who's got wind of my daughter's—endowments.

SILVIO: Cheap opportunist.

BRIGHELLA: I knew Signor Federigo in Turin.

LOMBARDI: A witness!

PANTALONE: Would you know him now in Venice?

BRIGHELLA: I'd know him anywhere.

BEATRICE: *(striding in)* Signor Pantalone!

PANTALONE: Sir!

BRIGHELLA: *(aside)* What?

BEATRICE: *(seeing Brighella)* Ah! *(recovering)* Sir! I do not wish to start off on the wrong foot, but I must protest your treatment of my servant. Your letters have been notable for their courtesy. Yet when I arrive in your great city, I find that my very veracity as to my very existence is called into question.

24

Moreover, I am faced with a servant so frightened and confused he is perhaps beyond retrieving— possibly unhinged.

LOMBARDI: I'll say.

BEATRICE: He wonders even as I speak to him if, in fact, I live and breathe.

PANTALONE: Excuse me, sir, but—

LOMBARDI: Spit it out.

PANTALONE: Who are you?

BEATRICE: Your servant, sir, Federigo Rasponi.

PANTALONE: Amazing!

CLARICE: Disastrous!

BRIGHELLA: *(aside)* Deceptive! Not Federigo, but his sister, Beatrice.

PANTALONE: Please understand, we all took the shocking news—we were shocked, deeply shocked, like Signor D'Amato at the Whitewater hearings, or Senator Packwood at his resignation ceremony— the shocking news, I say, of your death to heart. So when your servant announced your arrival, we couldn't make sense of his message. *(to Lombardi)* I'm not convinced.

BEATRICE: Yes, well, one can't believe all the gossip. I was only wounded, not killed. I am in fairly good shape, if I do say so myself—it takes more than a little flesh wound to put me down for the count. And after a miraculously quick convalescence, I set off for Venice, as we had arranged.

PANTALONE: Please, I hope you won't take this amiss, but, since I've had proof of your death—

25

LOMBARDI: Incontrovertible and categorically imperative evidence sine qua non!

PANTALONE: Uh—yes—well, you will sympathize with my need to have something—

LOMBARDI: Pertinent, relevant, and germane to the issue at hand, to wit: proof of your identity.

BEATRICE: Of course, nothing to it, I understand completely! *(whipping out impressively formal documents)* Letters from only the most official officials of Turin—

PANTALONE: *(taking documents, perusing them)* Biscotti.

BEATRICE: Indeed.

PANTALONE: Cassata.

BEATRICE: His son's my best friend.

PANTALONE: Zabaglione!

BEATRICE: He insisted.

PANTALONE: And Gelato!

BEATRICE: I have perhaps overdone it.

LOMBARDI: Let me see those! *(taking them)*

CLARICE: Silvio! We are undone!

SILVIO: Never!

LOMBARDI: Just as he says—Biscotti, Cassata, Zabaglione, Gelato! The crème de la crème caramel!

BEATRICE: They were glad to do it. *(to Brighella)* Excuse me, but I think I know you from somewhere else.

BRIGHELLA: You're right. Brighella Cavicchio—I used to run a small hotel in Turin.

BEATRICE: That's it—Brighella. And what brings you to Venice?

BRIGHELLA: Greener pastures. They're finally cleaning up the canal.

BEATRICE: *(aside)* Please—I'll explain—do not betray me.

BRIGHELLA: *(signaling acquiescence)* A new start with a new inn.

BEATRICE: Ah! You have room for me and my servant?

BRIGHELLA: I'd be honored. *(aside)* Smuggling something, I'll bet. Part of that tenacious olive oil cartel.

LOMBARDI: Logic is on his side. *(handing letters to Pantalone)*

PANTALONE: Indeed. This says that the bearer is Signor Rasponi, and you are the bearer.

LOMBARDI: Ergo.

PANTALONE: Ah, yes—we don't have to spell it out, do we?

CLARICE: C-a-t-a-s-t-r-o-f-e!

SILVIO: You are mine, mine, mine—we shall never part! *(nearly smothering her)*

BEATRICE: This must be your daughter, Clarice—although it is hard to tell.

PANTALONE: Yes, this is she. *(snatching her from Silvio, setting her to stand)* She's a little shy.

BEATRICE: *(of Silvio)* And this? A relative?

PANTALONE: Uh, yes—my—uh—nephew.

SILVIO: Please, sir! The truth will out! I, sir, am the freshly betrothed of Clarice, her promised husband until death!

BEATRICE: Oh?

LOMBARDI: Into the breach, m' boy—like a real man!

BEATRICE: I am increasingly bewildered.

LOMBARDI: *(to Silvio)* Nothing rash now.

BEATRICE: I traveled here under the apparently false impression that Signorina Clarice had been promised to me.

PANTALONE: Uh, well, yes, that's right.

BEATRICE: *(of Silvio)* Then—?

PANTALONE: I can explain.

LOMBARDI: You won't mind if I take notes. *(getting out writing materials)* Never hurts to take down hearsay while it's fresh.

PANTALONE: Once we had—recovered from the news of your death—

BEATRICE: I have told you, I—

PANTALONE: Yes, yes, please, let me finish. Since I thought, in all good faith—

LOMBARDI: *(writing)* Bona fides . . .

PANTALONE: —that you were dead, and since that condition is usually irrevocable, and since Signor Silvio here had submitted his own request, well! There was no impediment! I promised my daughter to him.

BEATRICE: That was then, but this is now.

LOMBARDI: *(writing)* Well said, precisely.

PANTALONE: No harm done! All membranes intact!

LOMBARDI: *(writing)* Virgo intacta, sed pulchra . . .

BEATRICE: Sir! A bit more subtle, if you please.

PANTALONE: Yes, sorry, I thought—well! You are here! She is here! Just in time, you can have her—assuming you still want her.

BEATRICE: Why wouldn't I want her? *(aside)* I'm going to enjoy this.

PANTALONE: What? Why, no reason, no reason, I've just explained! Uh—I'll keep my word and fork over the exorbitant dowry I promised—I mean, given your own affluence and position in Turin, it wasn't exorbitant, it just felt exorbitant. There is, shall we say, a perception of exorbitance. We'll deal with the details later, yes?

BEATRICE: As you wish.

PANTALONE: Signor Silvio, I can't tell you—

SILVIO: I'll bet you can't.

PANTALONE: Now, let's not get nasty. I couldn't possibly have known! Let's just forget the whole thing.

SILVIO: Forget! The most succulent woman in the world, rudely snatched from my grasp at this last possible moment! Hah! Besides, he doesn't really want damaged goods.

CLARICE: What!?

BEATRICE: I thought Signor Pantalone just said—

SILVIO: Her hymen may be intact—but her heart is compromised! She has promised herself to another—surely you won't force her to accept second best.

BEATRICE: Oh, I don't know about any forcing—but I don't mind. I quite understand the whole misunderstanding.

LOMBARDI: Oozing empathy!

BEATRICE: I hope Signorina Clarice will agree.

SILVIO: She will not agree, will you, dearest? She is mine, mine, mine!

LOMBARDI: Now, son, don't get possessive.

SILVIO: I will avenge myself, Signor Pantalone. Whoever presumes to take my Clarice will answer with drawn sword.

LOMBARDI: Go to, go to! Heh-heh!

BEATRICE: Only the good die young.

LOMBARDI: You are, sir, as my son says, too late. The law is crystal clear on this point. You get there first, you've staked the proper claim. Prior in tempore, potior in jure. Possession nine-tenths, and so on, and so on. We'll see you in court! *(he grabs Silvio, and they leave)*

BEATRICE: *(to Clarice)* And what do you say, Signorina?

CLARICE: I say—I say—*(bursts into tears, dashes off, wailing)*

PANTALONE: What? Ingrate! *(starting after her)* Impertinence!

BEATRICE: Please, Signor Pantalone, give her time to adjust. Meanwhile, we can go over our accounts.

PANTALONE: Are you just the teeniest bit concerned about your—pardon the expression—dowry money?

BEATRICE: Not at all.

PANTALONE: Because, if you are, let me—

BEATRICE: Please, there's no need—

PANTALONE: My reputation in these matters is beyond reproach. In fact, my own probity is held up as a model for householders and advertising executives, arbitragers and usurers, televangelists and nuns. Why, I have letters of recommendation from Signors Boesky, Milken, and Guy Bob Tucker, as well as Billy Cardinal Salivola and—

BEATRICE: If you prefer, we can do business later.

PANTALONE: Your money is ready whenever you like.

BEATRICE: As soon as I'm settled, I'll call on you.

PANTALONE: If you need the money now . . .

BEATRICE: Well, actually—

PANTALONE: Aha!

BEATRICE: A small advance on account—I was afraid to carry much cash, for fear of robbers along the way.

PANTALONE: I'll send a small advance straightaway to your lodgings. Even though the crime rate's been plummeting lately, there are still a few robbers left in Venice. Your servant. *(bowing)*

BEATRICE: *(returning the bow)* Sir.

(Pantalone leaves)

BRIGHELLA: I can't stand it another minute!

BEATRICE: Not so loud! *(checking on all sides)*

BRIGHELLA: Are we under surveillance?

BEATRICE: I need to maintain this disguise for a while yet. Please, be discreet.

31

BRIGHELLA: Don't tell me, let me guess: You killed your own brother and have assumed his identity so you can't be traced.

BEATRICE: Don't be absurd.

BRIGHELLA: You've found out you're gay, and you thought you might as well make a bid for Clarice before your brother tied the knot.

BEATRICE: You're raving.

BRIGHELLA: You've informed on the corrupt politicians of your fair city and have had to enter the federal witness protection program.

BEATRICE: Brighella! What's got into you?!

BRIGHELLA: I thought if I made up something really scandalous, you'd have to tell me the truth just to contain the fallout.

BEATRICE: The truth is really simple. My brother did die in a duel.

BRIGHELLA: You don't seem all that torn up about it.

BEATRICE: My brother brought it upon himself. He refused to grant his consent for me to marry. I loved my brother, but he was prone to greed. Florindo had little to offer. Worse, my brother wanted to present the best picture to Pantalone, in order to get the best dowry arrangement. If I married Florindo, my dowry would go with me, and my brother would have that much less to show in his accounts.

BRIGHELLA: It is a strain, being rich.

BEATRICE: It was either my brother, Federigo, or my lover, Florindo. I think you'd agree I made the right choice.

BRIGHELLA: Names are almost the same—that's confusing.

BEATRICE: Well, I wasn't confused about where my love and loyalty lay. Of course, Florindo—

BRIGHELLA: Your brother.

BEATRICE: My lover. Florindo had to flee Turin. My family is very well connected. When I heard he was headed for Venice, I borrowed my brother's clothes, packed his letters of credit, and followed. Once I draw the money from Signor Pantalone, I'll be better able to help Florindo.

BRIGHELLA: I thought he was dead.

BEATRICE: That's Federigo!

BRIGHELLA: Right, right, sorry.

BEATRICE: I'm sorry, I'm just a little stressed out, that's all. And I really appreciate your not giving me away. Oh, Brighella, you've got to help me, whatever lies ahead. I'll make it worth your while.

BRIGHELLA: I don't know. I'd rather not have to cross Signor Pantalone.

BEATRICE: We're just shading the truth a little. And it's only temporary. Once I find Florindo—

BRIGHELLA: He's the head of the Chamber of Commerce. I have to work with him.

BEATRICE: Oh, Brighella—you're one of the last people I'd expect to be scrupulous!

BRIGHELLA: I'm having an attack of ethics, I guess. I'm remapping my comfort zone.

BEATRICE: Look, it's only a short-term deception for a long-term good. Besides, since my brother's dead, I'm his heir.

BRIGHELLA: Then why not just come right out and say so?

BEATRICE: You of all people know the answer to that—because I'm female. Pantalone would go into his paternal mode. Or worse, his dirty-old-man act. Dealing with either one, I'd have to waste a lot of time and energy. This way, I can act freely and with dispatch. That's the whole reason playwrights invented these trouser roles anyway—to move the plot along. Only fair to let the female characters generate the action once in a while.

BRIGHELLA: I'm all for that! I'm not even supposed to have this part—traditionally, a man plays it—but I put my foot down! Give me a chance! I'll do it in drag if you want, but I deserve a chance to show my stuff. But you're already in drag—I guess that's why they let me play it as a woman. I mean, otherwise the audience'd get confused, and then where would we be? In a masterpiece! So there!

BEATRICE: Please, Brighella, say you'll help me. I guarantee it won't take long.

BRIGHELLA: Sisterhood is powerful, yes?

BEATRICE: All right!

(they exchange high and low fives)

BRIGHELLA: We are women!

BEATRICE: Hear us roar!

BRIGHELLA: Power to the women! The broads, the girls, the chicks!

BEATRICE: All is fair in love and war and sexual politics!

(they go into the inn as the lights fade)

Scene 2

TRUFFALDINO: My master's sure got a short memory. You think he's abandoned me in a strange city? I don't know what's worse. You hear stories about servants treated like slaves, under lock and key. At least they can raid the fridge once in a while. Here I've got the run of the city but not one cent in my pocket. And my belly's rumbling with hunger. *(to belly)* Keep it down, you're distracting me. For all I know, he could be long gone on his honeymoon, leaving me stuck and starving. Oh, what I'd give for something to swallow! Maybe I could swallow my pride and beg a little. Let my stomach rumblings pass for new age music! Be my own trumpet—now, there's a good trick. Or take up petty thievery, at least until I've pilfered some food. Maybe there's a convent nearby for indigent travelers? *(to his belly)* Quiet—I'm trying to think!

(groaning and scraping offstage)

(to belly) Now you're really overdoing it!

FLORINDO: *(entering)* Come now, just a few yards and we're there.

PORTER: *(following, groaning, dragging a trunk)* I'm a breath away from joining my dear dead mother, wherever she is. And I don't have any extra parts to spare. *(halting)* Like pulling a lead-lined coffin full of cement. I can't go another step.

TRUFFALDINO: *(to audience)* Ahah! This could be my next meal! *(to Florindo)* Excuse me, sir, allow me. *(easily picks up the trunk)*

FLORINDO: Ah—that's more like it.

TRUFFALDINO: A mere bagatelle, sir. *(to audience)* Whatever that is.

FLORINDO: Straight into the inn.

TRUFFALDINO: "Into the inn"—that's easy to remember. Piece of cake! *(turning, he knocks the porter down, enters the inn)*

PORTER: Agh! My poor old bones! Porters don't get workman's comp—I'll have to sue.

FLORINDO: *(flipping him a coin)* That's for your pains. *(starting in)*

PORTER: Nowhere near enough, sir.

FLORINDO: The landing's only ten yards off!

PORTER: And since you gave that fellow the order, you are liable for my injuries. Besides, even if I didn't sue—we've got a minimum.

FLORINDO: Minimum pay for minimum effort?

PORTER: Maximum effort.

FLORINDO: Minimum result.

PORTER: Do my best, sir.

FLORINDO: *(tossing another coin)* That should do it.

PORTER: Things're desperate, sir.

FLORINDO: Have you considered early retirement?

PORTER: Fine for you to say. What've you got t' retire from?

(Truffaldino emerges from the inn)

Fine man like you, wouldn't know how to earn your way.

FLORINDO: I'd never promise what I couldn't deliver.

TRUFFALDINO: This fellow bothering you, sir?

PORTER: And then we have riffraff coming in from all over.

TRUFFALDINO: Riffraff! *(takes up a menacing position)*

FLORINDO: That's enough, let it drop. *(handing Porter another coin)* Be off, now. They must have retraining programs in Venice—see if you can find a more suitable trade.

PORTER: See you in court. *(leaves)*

TRUFFALDINO: Grrrr—lemme at 'im. Riffraff! Just because I come from Bergamo! Really, sir, I have to thank you. I nearly let him have it. I can't stand being called names, and sometimes—well, I don't know my own strength.

FLORINDO: He was ready to keel over on his own.

TRUFFALDINO: In that case I could have killed him. Though I myself am not myself.

FLORINDO: Say what?

TRUFFALDINO: I myself am faint with hunger.

FLORINDO: Well, I wouldn't mind a bite.

TRUFFALDINO: This inn has the most mouthwatering smells coming from its kitchen. I've already charmed the waitress—you'll be treated like visiting royalty.

FLORINDO: You're in the restaurant business?

TRUFFALDINO: Me? Sir! The restaurant business! You're not serious! *(laughing)*

FLORINDO: Is that so ridiculous?

TRUFFALDINO: *(laughing still more)* Oh, I don't know. Maybe because—because—because—*(laughing)*

FLORINDO: Yes?

TRUFFALDINO: Because I'm always hungry!

FLORINDO: And?

TRUFFALDINO: And—if I had a restaurant—well—I'd be my own best customer, now, wouldn't I? I'd eat myself bankrupt!

FLORINDO: You have another trade, then?

TRUFFALDINO: I am, sir, a servant. From Bergamo. To the best of my ability, I serve. At your service, sir.

FLORINDO: And you are now gainfully employed?

TRUFFALDINO: To tell you the truth, sir, I am without a master. *(aside)* He's not here, so strictly speaking, my answer would pass muster on Court TV. Besides, maybe he is a ghost.

FLORINDO: A lucky coincidence. A master with no servant—

TRUFFALDINO: Let me guess. *(points to Florindo)*

FLORINDO: —meets a servant with no master.

TRUFFALDINO: Moi! I mean—

FLORINDO: Would you be interested in serving me?

TRUFFALDINO: Would I? *(suddenly playing hard to get)* Could be . . . could be. . . . Got a job description?

38

FLORINDO: The usual. Do what you're told, no questions asked. That sort of thing.

TRUFFALDINO: That's right up my alley, sir. My specialité, as they say. I never ask questions—they give me a headache. And why have a servant if he doesn't do what he's asked?

FLORINDO: What did your last master pay?

TRUFFALDINO: Oh, that's a tricky one, sir. He paid my room and board.

FLORINDO: No problem, fine.

TRUFFALDINO: You can't say I didn't warn you about my appetite.

FLORINDO: A hearty eater is a hard worker.

TRUFFALDINO: Uh—right, right. And of course, over and above that, I got—uh—four dollars an hour.

FLORINDO: Four dollars!

TRUFFALDINO: Plus tips, whenever they came my way.

FLORINDO: Whaat?!

TRUFFALDINO: Wasn't all that often.

FLORINDO: I don't know. It's a bit steep. And how do I know you're honest?

TRUFFALDINO: Look at me, sir. Do I look like an ax murderer?

FLORINDO: Ax murderer! Good lord! I didn't mean that! You're not an ax murderer, are you?

TRUFFALDINO: *(feigning dementia)* You never know, sir. Could be. Could be I chopped up my whole family and—

FLORINDO: Stop that! You're giving me the creeps!

TRUFFALDINO: Just kidding, sir. I can't even bring myself to smash a harmless fly. In fact I try to protect all the species, extinct or otherwise, from the perfidy—the preditoriousness—all the wiles and wherefores of humankind.

FLORINDO: What about references?

TRUFFALDINO: I've got piles.

FLORINDO: Good.

TRUFFALDINO: In Bergamo.

FLORINDO: No one in Venice—?

TRUFFALDINO: Just got here this morning.

FLORINDO: Well—what about a trial?

TRUFFALDINO: That means a lot of questions, sir—my head. All those legal terms! Habeas corpus, non compos mentis, flagrante delicti, loco parentis— and the initials! They are even more confusing! DNA, LAPD, O something—I don't think I could go through that, sir, even for as obvious a gentleman as you are, sir.

FLORINDO: Not a legal trial. We'll just try each other on, see how things go.

TRUFFALDINO: Yes, sir! *(saluting)* Your every wish!

FLORINDO: Here's your first job—see if there are any letters for Florindo Aretusi at the post office, and fetch them here at once.

TRUFFALDINO: Yes, sir! *(dashing off, suddenly halts)* And sir?

FLORINDO: Yes?

TRUFFALDINO: Shall I order dinner before I go?

FLORINDO: Letters first.

TRUFFALDINO: Yes, sir! *(dashing off, halts)* So.

FLORINDO: Now what?

TRUFFALDINO: So while I'm gone, you'll order dinner?

FLORINDO: *(laughing)* Fair enough. Right away. *(goes into inn)*

TRUFFALDINO: Well, I'd say things are definitely looking up. I was feeling suicidal a little while ago, and now—a new master, dinner on the way, and better wages than I've ever had in my life. I fudged the truth a little back there—I bet you guessed. I wasn't really making four dollars an hour with my last master. It was really half that—because I was going to get pretty sumptuous room and board. I'm sure my other master meant it—but he kept wandering off. Anyway! What's the difference now? I've got a new master—and he is ordering dinner!

(as Truffaldino starts out, he nearly collides with Beatrice, who enters with Brighella)

BEATRICE: Well! You nearly ran me down!

TRUFFALDINO: A thousand pardons, sir.

BEATRICE: And where have you been all this while? I thought you'd absconded.

TRUFFALDINO: You did? Well. Goodness. I'd never do a thing like that. Preposterous! No, sir. I was waiting for you.

BEATRICE: How was I supposed to know that?

41

TRUFFALDINO: Oh, I don't know, sir. You see, I did—
wander around a little—to distract myself from my
gastric concerns.

BEATRICE: Oh?

TRUFFALDINO: Exercise curbs the appetite.

BEATRICE: I'll curb your appetite.

TRUFFALDINO: You'll order dinner?

BEATRICE: After you haul my trunk from the landing.

TRUFFALDINO: Yes, sir. And where should I haul it?

BEATRICE: Why, here, of course.

TRUFFALDINO: Here?

BEATRICE: I am staying in Mistress Brighella's inn.

TRUFFALDINO: Oh, that's different. Or is it?

BEATRICE: Of course not. Get a move on, now. And
while you're at it, see if I have any letters at general
delivery. For me or my sister, Beatrice. I expect her
any day now.

TRUFFALDINO: *(aside)* Now what?!

BRIGHELLA: Letters for Beatrice? Isn't that a little
risky?

BEATRICE: My steward back home could use either
name—I forgot to instruct him. *(to Truffaldino)*
Are you still here? Get along!

(Brighella and she go into the inn)

TRUFFALDINO: This is what I get for complaining. First
I've got no master, then all of a sudden I've got
two! I can't wait on both of them—what to do,
what to do! How does it go? Last hired, first fired?
Applied to this situation, that means—that

42

means—that means—what, exactly does that mean? I owe first allegiance to my first master, because he hired me first. But my second master is paying me better. So it's in my best interest to serve him! Wait a minute, wait a minute, just . . . a . . . minute! Why can't I serve both? Get two pay packets, and eat and drink for two? Why not? That way, when the lean times come along, as they always do, I'll have something stashed away! And what if it didn't work out? I'd lose one job, but I'd still have the other! It's like two can live as cheaply as one, yes? Sort of. Right now, for instance, I'm going to the post for both of them—but I can do it in just one trip! I think I've stumbled onto something—and if I can make it work, why, maybe I'll open an employment agency!

(starting out, he nearly collides with Silvio)

SILVIO: Hey—watch where you're going!

TRUFFALDINO: Going? Going? I am going all the way to the top!! Just watch me!

SILVIO: I beg your pardon!

TRUFFALDINO: Oh, I'm sorry, sir—I was—daydreaming.

SILVIO: I'll say! Where's your master?

TRUFFALDINO: Uh—

SILVIO: Come on, come on—snap out of it.

TRUFFALDINO: *(doing so)* Yes, sir! Uh—he's in there. *(aside)* A twice-told truth, if ever there was one.

SILVIO: Please tell him Silvio Lombardi wishes to speak with him. I'll wait here.

TRUFFALDINO: But—

43

SILVIO: Hop to it!

TRUFFALDINO: I was just on my way—

SILVIO: Good.

TRUFFALDINO: —to the post office.

SILVIO: The post office can wait.

TRUFFALDINO: You're right. That's all I ever do when I'm there. Sometimes I think they're in a time zone all their own—or else on downers. What do you think?

SILVIO: Are you going to get your master, or do I have to get him myself?

TRUFFALDINO: In fact, I've got a theory about all those serial killers who've lost their jobs at the post office and come back one morning and blast the place to kingdom come. First, they're in Valium withdrawal, they're not responsible. And second—

SILVIO: Fetch your master!

TRUFFALDINO: *(aside)* But—which one?

SILVIO: Maybe you'd like a little push?

TRUFFALDINO: No, no, I'm on my way, only take a second. *(aside)* Whichever one I find first. *(goes in)*

SILVIO: Arrghn! I'm sooo pissed off! That Federigo'd better give up any claim to Clarice, or I'll fight him to the death—his! Insolent little pipsqueak! He'll wish he'd died when he was supposed to!

TRUFFALDINO: *(entering with Florindo)* Over there, sir. I've got to run—the post office'll be closing soon.

FLORINDO: Sir?

SILVIO: Sir?

FLORINDO: You asked for me?

SILVIO: There must be some mistake. I told him I wanted his master.

FLORINDO: I am his master.

SILVIO: Then I owe you an apology. Either your servant has a twin, or he's got two masters.

FLORINDO: He's got only one master—me.

SILVIO: Then who is serving Federigo Rasponi?

FLORINDO: Federigo Rasponi?

SILVIO: You know him?

FLORINDO: I did. Unfortunately.

SILVIO: A man after my own heart. This Federigo claims the woman who swore to be my wife only this morning.

FLORINDO: That's impossible. Federigo Rasponi is dead.

SILVIO: So we all thought. And then, this morning, there he is, newly arrived in Venice, hale and hearty and headed for the altar—with my betrothed!

FLORINDO: Then he has been resurrected.

SILVIO: My fiancée's father, Signor Pantalone dei Bisognosi, no fool he, has checked it out. Swears he's the genuine article. Well, I can swear too. And by God! one of us will either give up Clarice, or give up the ghost! He was supposed to be staying at this inn. *(Florindo does an innocent take)* If you see him, tell him Silvio Lombardi is looking for him. Sir!

45

FLORINDO: Sir! *(Silvio strides off)* I had word he died. But it's true, I left in such a rush, maybe he did miraculously recover. So is that good news, or bad? Is he following me here because he's had a change of heart? Or because he still opposes my marrying Beatrice? Beloved Beatrice. How I have missed her! *(pulls out her portrait, falls into a reverie)* And you, beloved? Are you pining for me, as I for you? Or have you already, as women are wont to do, found solace in the sinuous arms of another? Oh! The very thought propels me into the depths of despair! Spent like spilt water! I can hardly hold up my head to hope that one day, all will be well and you will be mine!

TRUFFALDINO: Hurry up, and—

(Leading a second Porter, who carries Beatrice's trunk, Truffaldino stops dead at seeing Florindo. Panicked, he frantically waves the Porter back and speaks in a stage whisper.) Back, back! *(the Porter disappears)*

FLORINDO: This imperfect image, however distant from the excellent reality, nevertheless imparts enough of a hint of your charms that my thirst for you is partly slaked, even as I long for more, more, more!

TRUFFALDINO: Uh, sir . . .

FLORINDO: I am impatient for the day that brings me news of your continued constancy.

TRUFFALDINO: Speaking of constancy, sir, here I am. And with news to boot!

FLORINDO: You've got my letters?

TRUFFALDINO: Of course, of course, nothing to it. *(pulls out three letters, then realizes he does not know one from another)*

FLORINDO: Goodness! Three!

TRUFFALDINO: Uh, yes, well, they're not all for you.

FLORINDO: Oh?

TRUFFALDINO: Uh, yes, uh, you see, on my way to the post office I met another servant I used to work with in Bergamo, and he asked me to see if there was anything for his master, and so I did, and so there was, but—but—since I can't read, I forget which one it is.

FLORINDO: No problem—I'll take mine and give you the other.

TRUFFALDINO: Yes, sir, well, we servants like to do each other a good turn once in a while, seeing as how most of the rest of the world doesn't give a damn one way or the other about us, and—

FLORINDO: What?! Beatrice Rasponi? Here?

TRUFFALDINO: If you've finished sorting the mail, sir, I'll take it to—

FLORINDO: Who is this other fellow?

TRUFFALDINO: Uh—a servant—

FLORINDO: So you said. His name.

TRUFFALDINO: Uh—uh—Pasqual'.

FLORINDO: His master's name.

TRUFFALDINO: Uh—I don't know, sir.

FLORINDO: How could you fetch his master's letters if you didn't know his master's name?

TRUFFALDINO: How could I fetch his master's letters if I didn't know his master's name? Good question. Uh—I forgot his master's name. I mean, I didn't

47

actually know it. Pasqual' wrote it down on a bit of paper, and I just handed it over to the postmaster.

FLORINDO: Let me see the paper.

TRUFFALDINO: *(making a show of searching his pockets)* Hm—not there. Hmm—not there, either. Must've left it at the post. Sorry. *(aside)* Just going with the flow.

FLORINDO: Where does Pasqual' live?

TRUFFALDINO: No idea.

FLORINDO: Well, how are you supposed to give him this letter?

TRUFFALDINO: He was—he was—meeting me in the piazza. Now, if you'll just give that to me. *(snatches for the letter, but Florindo puts it out of reach)* Sir—that does not belong to you!

FLORINDO: I'm not going to keep it—I just want to read it.

TRUFFALDINO: Sir! I am shocked! Deeply shocked! And troubled—deeply, deeply troubled. It is against the law to open other people's letters.

FLORINDO: Actually, I know the addressee.

TRUFFALDINO: *(aside)* Then why did he ask me his name?

FLORINDO: I have that person's best interest at heart. I can open this letter without a qualm. *(with a flourish, he opens it)*

TRUFFALDINO: *(as if run through)* Ah! He opened it!

FLORINDO: *(reading)* "Signorina Beatrice—Your family prevails. The Court of Justice intends to have you arrested for having absconded with your brother's letters of credit. I have sent this letter via Genoa so as to conceal your whereabouts. I will keep you posted. Your faithful servant, Antonio."

TRUFFALDINO: Any second now the police will arrest him. I mean, hasn't he ever heard the word superstitious? I mean, supercilious? I mean, surreptitious?

FLORINDO: Beatrice here! Truffaldino!

TRUFFALDINO: Sir! Not so loud!

FLORINDO: Quick! Find Pasqual'—

TRUFFALDINO: Who's Pasqual? Oh—oh—you mean Pasqual'!

FLORINDO: Isn't that what I said? Bring him to me— I'll make it well worth your while.

TRUFFALDINO: I'll need the letter.

FLORINDO: Here.

TRUFFALDINO: And how'm I to explain it's been opened?

FLORINDO: A simple mistake. You forgot and gave them all to your master, and he just opened them automatically, not realizing, and so forth, and so forth. But hurry! *(aside)* Beatrice and Federigo, both here! I must find her before he does! *(dashing off)*

TRUFFALDINO: This is some pickle I'm in. Ooh— wouldn't a pickle taste good right now? Hold on, Truff, pull yourself together! I can't tell my other master I gave his letter to this master! I'll just have to put it back the way it was. *(tries various options)* Well, not exactly—but it'll have to do. My grandmother seals letters with bread—I have to give up

49

my last morsel, but it's in a good cause. Besides, dinner should be almost ready. *(puts bread in his mouth, enjoys it for a moment, automatically swallows it)* Oh, no! I mean, it's delicious, but I'm not getting the job done. *(repeat business)* It's fate. One more time. *(this time, after a great struggle, he takes the bread from his mouth)* That's will power for you! Now. *(meticulously seals the letter, then suddenly pounds it closed)* Take that! Well! Looks even better now than it did before—unless I'm thinking of the other two letters. Well, what's the difference! This one's fit for a signet ring!

PORTER: *(dragging trunk, enters)* Coast clear? I get time and a half, you know.

TRUFFALDINO: Whoops! Forgot all about you.

PORTER: Well, thanks a lot. Where d' you want this?

TRUFFALDINO: Uh—right in there.

(as Porter starts toward inn, Beatrice appears in the doorway)

BEATRICE: My trunk!

PORTER: *(handing her a slip of paper)* My bill.

BEATRICE: Don't worry—I'm good for it.

PORTER: You'd better be. *(grumbling as he goes in)* Wasted half the afternoon, missed how many jobs, don't know what's—

BEATRICE: Any letters?

TRUFFALDINO: Just this one—for your sister.

BEATRICE: *(snatching it)* It's been opened!

TRUFFALDINO: No!

BEATRICE: Yes! And sealed with bread!

TRUFFALDINO: Amazing!

BEATRICE: Truffaldino, if you know anything about this—

TRUFFALDINO: Me?

BEATRICE: Don't lie to me!

TRUFFALDINO: I confess! Please, sir, don't beat me!

BEATRICE: Hurry up!

TRUFFALDINO: It's my fault. Nobody's perfect, right? At least, not in this vale of tears. Truth is, at the post office, there was a letter for me. I get so few, I was totally excited. Only—well—I don't read much, so instead of opening my letter, I opened yours. Illiteracy always leads to ill fortune.

BEATRICE: Well, no harm, then. You didn't read it.

TRUFFALDINO: How could I?

BEATRICE: Did anyone else—?

TRUFFALDINO: Pul-leeze.

BEATRICE: Truffaldino.

TRUFFALDINO: How can you even suggest—?

BEATRICE: Very well. *(reading)*

TRUFFALDINO: *(to audience)* That was a close one.

BEATRICE: I have a few things to take care of with Signor Pantalone. Here. *(hands keys to him)* Unpack my trunk. As soon as I come back, we'll have dinner. *(leaves)*

TRUFFALDINO: *(to audience)* You see? You just think as fast as you can, and it turns out to be good enough. One dinner ordered, a second coming! Am I in heaven, or what?

51

PANTALONE: *(entering)* Ah! What luck! Is your master home, Truffaldino?

TRUFFALDINO: Not yet, sir, far as I know. *(to audience)* I think.

PANTALONE: Well, when he arrives, will you give him this purse? *(handing it over)* That small advance we spoke about—a paltry thousand dollars. I don't want to be rude, but I've got lots of business to take care of now that your master is marrying my daughter. I'm sure he'll understand. *(leaves)*

TRUFFALDINO: Which master, I wonder.

FLORINDO: *(entering)* Back already? Did you meet Pasqual'?

TRUFFALDINO: Uh, unfortunately, no. He may have misunderstood me. Or he could be expecting me after dinner. Pasqual' doesn't like to go out before he's had his dinner.

FLORINDO: What good are you if—

TRUFFALDINO: But! I met a man who gave me this purse of a thousand dollars.

FLORINDO: What? Whatever for?

TRUFFALDINO: Whoever for, you mean. Tell me, were you expecting a small advance?

FLORINDO: As a matter of fact, I did present a letter of credit to a banker this afternoon. For exactly that amount—why?

TRUFFALDINO: Oh, ah, no reason. Except—

FLORINDO: Out with it.

TRUFFALDINO: The fellow who gave me this purse said it was for my master.

FLORINDO: Well, what's all the delay, then? Who could he have meant but me?

TRUFFALDINO: Uh, nobody, I guess, sir. *(hands over the purse)*

FLORINDO: *(counting the money)* You'll check in with Pasqual' right away now.

TRUFFALDINO: After dinner.

FLORINDO: *(laughing)* All right, all right. We'll order right now. *(going in)*

TRUFFALDINO: Well, that was a close one! Nothing like being sure. Trust, but verify. *(going in)*

Scene 3

Pantalone leads Clarice by the hand, Smeraldina follow-ing. Clarice has buried her face in a handkerchief, and in-termittently sniffles and yowls.

PANTALONE: You must surrender to the inevitable, my dear. There's nothing to be done. If you think all of this carrying on is going to make any differ-ence, you'd better think again.

CLARICE: Oh, Father! How can you be so cruel?

PANTALONE: Oh, daughter—how can you be so head-strong?

CLARICE: You know I have obeyed you in everything.

PANTALONE: Well, good, I'm glad to be reminded— keep it up, keep it up. You'd better dry your tears—Signor Rasponi will be here any moment. I don't want him changing his mind when he sees your red and swollen face.

CLARICE: *(to audience)* Now there's an idea.

53

SMERALDINA: He's coming, Signorina. Oh, you look terrible—I mean, here, let me—uh—freshen you up a little. *(doing so)*

CLARICE: Oh, Smeraldina, I am so miserable.

SMERALDINA: Coraggio, Signorina—he's not all that bad. Why, if you and I could trade places—

CLARICE: Oh, Smeraldina—would you?!

SMERALDINA: Signorina! Don't talk nonsense. All I mean is, he's quite a catch. If we belonged to the same—world—and if he had the desire—well, I'd be honored to be his wife. He's dashing, witty, and has a certain . . . je ne sais quoi. I can't quite put my finger on it, but he has a definite aura.

CLARICE: But I love Silvio.

SMERALDINA: Well, you can't always get what you want. *(launching into Mick Jagger)* "But you get what you neeeed!"

PANTALONE: Clarice, be realistic. This—situation—is nobody's fault. But Federigo has a prior claim.

CLARICE: *(wailing)* Oh, Father! I was reconciled—completely—obediently—just as a dutiful daughter like I ought to be—to marrying Federigo. I had stamped out the passionate flames of my feeling for Silvio—I had strangled the voice of longing rising in my delicate throat—I had trampled into stony ground the shoots of esteem and affection I had been cultivating in my heart. Father wants it, I shall do it.

PANTALONE: Exactly, exactly.

CLARICE: But—

PANTALONE: Eh?

CLARICE: —when you told me of Federigo's death, when you agreed that Silvio and I could be betrothed, ah, then! My heart blossomed! My voice sang out! My blood kindled into a fiery furnace ablaze with flames of feeling, athrob with the pulsations of—

SMERALDINA: *(to audience)* She does go on.

CLARICE: Anticipating a destined fusion with my one and only fated love!

PANTALONE: That was before, this is after.

CLARICE: Oh, you have said the word—after! After the light has faded! After the sun has set! After the warmth of summer has waned! After the ice of winter has frozen my heart!

SMERALDINA: Mistress, please, you'll make yourself sick.

CLARICE: Oh, I already feel as if I am at death's door, Smeraldina. I cannot face Federigo now!

SMERALDINA: *(leading her to a bench)* Here—sit down. I'll get you something to drink. *(going into the inn as Beatrice comes out)*

BEATRICE: Ah—Signor Pantalone—and your lovely daughter.

PANTALONE: Yes, well, not so lovely at the moment. She finds this—adjustment—a bit—rigorous.

BEATRICE: Of course, of course. I do understand. No need to rush anything.

(Smeraldina returns, and serves Clarice)

PANTALONE: You have received my advance? Found everything in order?

BEATRICE: No, no—you left it with my servant?

PANTALONE: I certainly did!

BEATRICE: I haven't seen him lately—I'm sure there's no problem.

PANTALONE: I should hope not. Though I have no proof that what I say is true—for all you know, I could be making this up, only to accuse your servant later of having absconded with the funds.

BEATRICE: That's absurd.

PANTALONE: Or worse, perhaps, he could be found dead in the street, his pockets turned inside out, not a dollar of my advance to be found! And then where would I be?

BEATRICE: Signor Pantalone, I trust you.

PANTALONE: *(to audience)* He does?

BEATRICE: And I trust Truffaldino.

PANTALONE: I don't know—servants can deceive even the wisest, sharpest-eyed masters.

BEATRICE: Please—do not concern yourself.

PANTALONE: Just so everything's out in the open. Some people think I'm a sharper, a skinflint—

BEATRICE: No!

PANTALONE: Exactly, Signor Rasponi—exactly! We are of one mind.

BEATRICE: Indeed.

PANTALONE: Meanwhile, my daughter—I'm afraid I haven't been entirely successful in persuading her of our current course. Perhaps you could . . . ?

BEATRICE: I'll try my best.

PANTALONE: *(to Clarice)* I am called away for the moment, my dear. Federigo will entertain you.

CLARICE: Oh, Fa—

PANTALONE: *(stopping her mouth)* Delighted, of course. *(sotto voce)* Don't do or say anything—assertive. *(to Beatrice)* Arrivederci! Smeraldina—please attend out of earshot. They are not yet betrothed; still, they need a bit of privacy.

BEATRICE: Signorina Clarice—

CLARICE: Stand back! Do not touch me!

BEATRICE: Believe me, Signorina, I have no desire to offend you.

CLARICE: Offend me! Your very existence offends me! Oh, if only you had died! How I wish you had!

BEATRICE: Signorina! Isn't that a little—extreme?

CLARICE: As for me, I might as well be dead. Doomed forever to be wed to one for whom I feel not the slightest ardor. While the one upon whom I have bestowed my heart totally must languish and pine from now until eternity in a prison built by Dame Fortune's caprice! Bereft of his beloved! As I, bereft of mine!

BEATRICE: Well, when you put it that way . . .

CLARICE: Beat me! Starve me! Put me out in a freezing snowstorm! Deny me all creature comforts! Shelter me from civilized society! Forbid me to shop! I shall never, ever relent in my resolve to spurn your advances!

BEATRICE: Signorina, I—

CLARICE: Stop hassling me!

BEATRICE: But I—

CLARICE: Every syllable from your mouth tortures my shellpink ears!

BEATRICE: If you would listen for a moment—

CLARICE: Has any woman suffered the outrageous affront I now am made to suffer?

SMERALDINA: *(who has heard every word)* Please, Signorina—chill out a little.

CLARICE: Okay—I was running out of words anyway. But I warn you, Signor Rasponi, whatever you say, you'll never alter my determination to love Silvio until that unfortunately faraway day when I shuffle off this mortal coil, and am united with him in heaven.

BEATRICE: Maybe you won't have to wait that long.

CLARICE: Go ahead, kill me. I'd rather be dead than—

BEATRICE: Just hear me out, please. What I have to say will relieve your misery.

CLARICE: Never! Never, never, nev—

SMERALDINA: Signorina! Give him a chance!

CLARICE: What for?

SMERALDINA: I think there's more to him than meets the eye.

BEATRICE: Or less, perhaps.

CLARICE: Riddles. And I already have a headache that incapacitates me!

BEATRICE: May I speak to the point?

SMERALDINA: What a relief!

CLARICE: Whatever you say is pointless.

BEATRICE: At the risk of being blunt: you don't want to marry me.

SMERALDINA: In a nutshell.

BEATRICE: And I don't want to marry you.

CLARICE: What! You should count yourself lucky.

BEATRICE: And so I would, if I were he who I seem. However—

CLARICE: More riddles?

BEATRICE: In addition, you have promised your hand to another, and so have I.

CLARICE: Ah—so we're in this together?

BEATRICE: Moreover—

SMERALDINA: Like most men, he does know how to prolong the agony, doesn't he? At this rate, a woman might prefer premature ejaculation. Let's get it over with!

BEATRICE: I am not Federigo—I am his sister, Beatrice.

SMERALDINA: I knew he was too good to be true.

CLARICE: I hope this isn't your idea of a joke.

BEATRICE: On the contrary, it is very serious business. So serious that I must have your word of honor not to reveal my secret until I allow it.

SMERALDINA: Maybe I should consider a sex change.

CLARICE: You'll let me tell Silvio.

BEATRICE: No one. You, too, Smeraldina—not one word to another soul, or my own plans may be put

59

in jeopardy. You see, my own lover, Florindo, killed my brother in a duel. Until I find Florindo, I must maintain my disguise.

CLARICE: I want to tell Silvio.

BEATRICE: He'll be the better man for having suffered a little longer. And really—if the truth gets out, my life is over. If I am discovered, my uncle will lock me up in a convent.

CLARICE: A fate worse than death!

BEATRICE: Our secret. *(all three clasp hands)* If it was good enough for Hamlet, it's good enough for us. *(in a ghostly voice)* "Sweeeaaarr."

SMERALDINA & CLARICE: We do so sweeeaarr.

BEATRICE: Sisterhood is powerful.

CLARICE: Painful.

SMERALDINA: And devious.

BEATRICE: I hope you'll treat me with a little more kindness, Clarice.

CLARICE: I will try to trust you.

BEATRICE: You doubt me? Here—I will prove what I say. Embrace me.

(Pantalone enters)

CLARICE: *(reluctantly doing so)* Ah. Yes, indeed—you are a woman.

PANTALONE: What's this? What's this? Once a father turns his back! No matter, no matter—my dear, you are transformed.

CLARICE: Well, I—

PANTALONE: Smeraldina, there's work to do. We've got a wedding to give!

SMERALDINA: *(to audience)* Uh-oh.

PANTALONE: Quick, quick, no need to drag things out! They're compounding interest daily now, you know.

BEATRICE: Well, sir, we're in no rush.

PANTALONE: You seemed to be just now. I don't want any scandal. All my grandchildren will be legitimate! Andiamo!

BEATRICE: What about our financial arrangements?

PANTALONE: A few minutes, an hour at most—nothing to delay over.

CLARICE: But this is too sudden, Father! Oh! *(to audience)* I'm even worse off than before.

SMERALDINA: What about Silvio?

PANTALONE: Yes, yes, of course, he has his pride. I'll go to him at once, explain everything.

CLARICE: Please, Father—don't upset him.

PANTALONE: He'll just have to like it or lump it, child. What's the difference? What is Silvio to you now, or you to Silvio?

CLARICE: Well, I just don't want to hurt him—heedlessly.

PANTALONE: I don't understand—bigamy's a crime in Venice. If you've decided for Federigo, what do you care about Silvio?

CLARICE: I guess I'm just a softie at heart, Father. Please—just be—sensitive to his feelings.

PANTALONE: Goes without saying. *(starting off)*

BEATRICE: You might want to wait a couple of days.

PANTALONE: Whatever for?

BEATRICE: Oh, I don't know—invitations?

PANTALONE: More mouths to feed. Am I made of money? No, no, these small, intimate, spontaneous weddings are much better. Besides, after what I saw the two of you doing—I am taking no chances! You think I want a grandson with no inheritance? Come along, Smeraldina—we'll go over the menu. *(leaving)*

SMERALDINA: *(to audience)* That should take two minutes. *(leaving)*

CLARICE: *(taking Beatrice's hand)* Oh, Beatrice! Now what?

PANTALONE: *(rushing back, grabbing Clarice)* Enough of that, enough! *(to Beatrice)* Control yourself, sir! Pazienza! Andiamo, andiamo—arrivederci, Federigo.

BEATRICE: Now what? Oh, why does the course of love have to run so rocky? Sometimes, I wish I'd never set eyes on Florindo.

(Florindo appears in her mind's eye)

FLORINDO: It was love at first sight.

BEATRICE: By the glimmering moon . . .

FLORINDO: When I glimpsed her that night—

BEATRICE: God gave me a boon.

FLORINDO: She at her window—

BEATRICE: As I gazed on Florindo . . .

62

FLORINDO: I on the ground.

BEATRICE: My heart whirled around.

FLORINDO: As if it were happening this very moment! As I gaze on her portrait—pale, imperfect likeness!—I conjure her fully rounded, cheeks fresh as roses, eyes flashing sapphires.

BEATRICE: I was drawn to him as the drifting ship to the beacon light. Blessed by fortune, I had found my way home.

FLORINDO: Even more precious than her beauty, her goodness. And courage in the face of her greedy brother's opposition.

BEATRICE: His patience in adversity.

FLORINDO: Oh! Coraggio! *(fading out)*

BEATRICE: Ah! Pazienza! *(fading out)*

Scene 4

Lombardi rushes on from one side as Pantalone rushes on from the other. They nearly collide.

LOMBARDI: Coincidence! I was just going to your house!

PANTALONE: And I to yours! Coincidence indeed.

LOMBARDI: After you.

PANTALONE: After you.

LOMBARDI: You first.

PANTALONE: No, no, please.

LOMBARDI: After all, as the father of the bride.

PANTALONE: So learned and respected a man as you—

LOMBARDI: You have a point.

PANTALONE: Well, when you put it that way.

LOMBARDI: The problem is—

PANTALONE: To put it plain—

LOMBARDI: You're legally bound.

PANTALONE: The deal's off.

LOMBARDI: What?

PANTALONE: Be realistic.

LOMBARDI: A contract's a contract.

PANTALONE: Is it my fault we got false information?

LOMBARDI: Not germane, irrelevant, a red herring that's beside the point.

PANTALONE: My dear sir—

LOMBARDI: In addition to having an airtight case, we do not want this—little dispute—to degenerate into a courtroom brawl replete with barbed innuendo and sarcastic allusions. Both Silvio and I are willing to forgive and forget.

PANTALONE: Well, I guess I'm glad to hear that.

LOMBARDI: You were reacting in the heat of the moment, as surprised as all of us, and gored on the horns of a dilemma.

PANTALONE: Well, that's true, I'd no idea—

LOMBARDI: Precisely. Quick as you are—

PANTALONE: Why, thank you.

LOMBARDI: —you weren't quick enough to distinguish between your promise to Signor Rasponi and your promise to my son and to me.

PANTALONE: Well, actually, I think I can distin—

LOMBARDI: Moreover, your promise is compounded in force and magnitude by your daughter's promise. What precedes in time has been supplanted by what follows because of its superior strength and enforceability.

PANTALONE: I wouldn't say—

LOMBARDI: Ergo: there is, as they say, no problem. Where marriage is concerned, consensus, et non concubitus, facit virum.

PANTALONE: Well, I'm no expert in ancient languages—

LOMBARDI: Take my word for it. I am. Though maybe it's not virum, maybe it's verum. I'll have to check—a niggling point, but nevertheless—

PANTALONE: Yes, well—uh, you've said your say?

LOMBARDI: I have.

PANTALONE: Basically presented your argument.

LOMBARDI: Completely.

PANTALONE: I may safely get a word in?

LOMBARDI: Absolutely. Carry on.

PANTALONE: I disagree there's no prob—

LOMBARDI: Of course, as far as the dowry is concerned, a bit of compensation might be in order, although we will not press the point if—

PANTALONE: It's my turn!!

LOMBARDI: All right, all right, don't get apoplectic!

PANTALONE: The legal point is irrelevant.

LOMBARDI: Impossible. Unless your daughter has decided to marry Signor Rasponi?

PANTALONE: She has. The whole situation is regrettable, but—what can I tell you?

LOMBARDI: You can tell me she's keeping her prior promise. You can tell me she's marrying my son.

PANTALONE: Doctor Lombardi, may I be frank?

LOMBARDI: Eh?

PANTALONE: You consider yourself a father.

LOMBARDI: I am a father.

PANTALONE: Ah—but you have only a son.

LOMBARDI: The son is preferable, we all know that. The son is superior in every way. The son carries on the father's work, inherits the father's wealth, propagates the father's grandchildren. The son—

PANTALONE: Yes, yes, and so on, as you might say. But—it is the daughter who tests the mettle of the father, far beyond any challenge posed by the son. It is the daughter who tries the father's soul, and puts salt in the father's gelato, and gall in the father's zuppa. Do you think if I could change her tiny mind I would not do my utmost? In fact I have used every ruse, assayed every strategy, cajoled, whined, intimidated, and inveighed, all to no avail. If you had a daughter, you would understand. What's more, you would commiserate, and not, as you now do, threaten me with legalistic maxims and vengeful retaliations. Well! I hope I have made myself clear and that you will be persuaded of my position.

LOMBARDI: Are you finished?

PANTALONE: Quite, yes, thank you.

LOMBARDI: You're sure?

PANTALONE: Not a doubt about it.

LOMBARDI: Allow me, then, and please do not interrupt until I finish.

PANTALONE: I wouldn't think of—

LOMBARDI: Silentium! All this nonsense about daughters doesn't concern me one whit. If you can't control your daughter, that's your deficiency, misfortune, and incompetence. You have been entirely too permissive in her upbringing—no doubt you followed Dr. Spockatini—and now the chickens are coming home to roost. No matter. What does matter is that you failed to verify Fedrigo Rasponi's death before you promised your daughter to my son! You could have asked for a death certificate. You could have required an open casket. You could have demanded sworn statements verifying his demise from the funeral director, or his father confessor. But did you do any of these perfectly reasonable things? Nooo! No, no, no, no, no. Stupid, negligent, careless, wanton, foolish fellow!

PANTALONE: But—but—but—

LOMBARDI: I AM NOT FINISHED!!! As if these sins of omission weren't enough, you expect you can simply toss off your agreement with my son! Even if Signor Rasponi were to reappear—

PANTALONE: As he—

LOMBARDI: AS HE HAS, YES!!! As he has reappeared! You would have been well within your right, not to mention your obligation to my son, to point out that when news of Rasponi's death reached us, it arrived not as a hypothetical, but as a given, a certainty, beyond the most reasonable or unreasonable of doubts. Such conditions warranted your assumption that you were freed of your earlier obligation, and, that, given these circumstances, he hadn't a leg to stand on.

PANTALONE: But he has—

LOMBARDI: —I speak figuratively, of course, of course, he has two perfectly good legs, DO NOT INTERRUPT ME!!! This very afternoon, before witnesses! *(flourishing documents)* My son and your daughter promised union until death! You expect us just to roll over and play dead when you announce you have yet another contract with this resurrected interloper, and that these instruments of the law are simply to be overlooked, set aside, or even, heaven help us, shredded?! Hah! Hah! You know not with whom you trifle, Signor Pantalone, you know not! And at your peril, my dear sir, at your peril you ignore my family's good name and influence throughout the republic of Venice and on into Lombardy, Tuscany, the Amalfi Coast, and the Papal States! What God hath joined together, let no man put asunder! Now! You may wonder if I have in mind to insist upon an annulment of this contract with Rasponi. I must confess, my son wishes us to take that course, for he is still determined to marry your daughter, despite her apparent willingness to flip from pillar to post, as all of these young people do, and go off with the next handsome face who happens to have a good name and plenty of money. However! I have myself had second thoughts about allying my family with yours—a family whose word is not its bond, a family that regards obligation as a trifling whim,

68

duty as mere gossamer caprice. Mark my word, sir, mark my word! The day will come, I see it looming in the shadows, sub specie aeternitatis, when the powers above and the civil republic here below will require compensation for this affront foisted upon the house of Lombardi! Tempus fugit, yes! Vivat misericordia, sed quoque justitia! Et justitia triumphat! *(leaves in high dudgeon)*

PANTALONE: I wish he would stop throwing Latin in my face. It's so old-fashioned! He's just trying to intimidate people with excessive displays of erudition. And, since I barely understand a word, for all I know he could be speaking vulgarisms! Windbag! Pedant! Partner in the law firm of Bluster, Muster and Booby! You know where you can put all that hot air! Should I be trembling in my slippers? Hah! I don't give a flea's eyelash for your flimflam. Why, the Rasponis outshine the Lombardis as the sun the moon, outclass the Lombardis as the Doge a two-bit local pol!! The house of Lombardi! Hah! More like a hut.

SILVIO: *(entering)* Sir!

PANTALONE: Sir!

SILVIO: My father has just informed me of your decision.

PANTALONE: Mine, yes, but my daughter concurs.

SILVIO: I cannot believe that. And for the moment, your daughter is irrelevant.

PANTALONE: She will be relieved to hear that.

SILVIO: It is you, sir, you upon whom I now vent my bilious spleen.

PANTALONE: Oh, dear!

SILVIO: You are no man of honor.

PANTALONE: Watch yourself now.

SILVIO: Your word is not your bond, sir, your reputation isn't worth a spoiled fig, and you left your integrity long ago when you lost your youth and virility.

PANTALONE: Now just a minute! I have not lost my—vigor!

SILVIO: Then you are perhaps in a mood to accept a young man's challenge? I have a mind to run you through right here!

PANTALONE: Hah! I'm no suckling pig to be spitted for your pleasure! You err, sir, in dissing me!

SILVIO: Opportunist!

PANTALONE: Twerp!

SILVIO: Skinflint!

PANTALONE: Dweeb!

SILVIO: Eunuch!

PANTALONE: Pipsqueak!

SILVIO: *(drawing his sword)* I swear to heaven, I shall defend my honor!

PANTALONE: *(drawing a pistol)* And I mine, you—

BEATRICE: *(rushing)* Wait! Hold! *(to Pantalone)* Put up your pistol, I shall protect you!

SILVIO: Fine by me—you're the man I really want to shishkabob!

BEATRICE: *(to audience)* Wish me luck! I did fit in a couple of lessons before I fled Turin.

SILVIO: Come on, come on, let's go!

BEATRICE: You've met your match, Signor. *(to audience)* I can't afford to lose—I have too much at stake.

PANTALONE: *(running off, calling)* Help! Consiglieri! Murder! Mayhem! Help!

BEATRICE: *(strikes)* Take that!

SILVIO: Take that!

BEATRICE: And that!

SILVIO: And that!

BEATRICE: And that, and that, and that!!

(Silvio falls, drops his sword. Beatrice places her point on his chest.)

CLARICE: *(dashing in)* Wait! No! Cease, desist, and stop!

BEATRICE: *(to audience)* Her father's daughter! For you, sweet Signorina Clarice, I will spare this young pup's life. *(putting up her sword)* And in return for this gesture, dropping gentle rain from heaven, I caution you to remember your oath and to honor it. *(leaves)*

CLARICE: Dearest Silvio! Are you all right?

SILVIO: Who wants to know?

CLARICE: You're delirious. Don't you recognize me? I am your loving Clarice!

SILVIO: My faithless Clarice! My loving Clarice is no more! She has rejected my love, she has spurned my suit, she has betrayed me for another, oh, cruel fate!

CLARICE: Please, Silvio, your words cut my heart to ribbons. I love you more than ever! I worship you! I will be faithful until the end of time, till the poets run out of rhyme, till the seas run dry and the sun goes dark and—

SILVIO: Save it.

CLARICE: Silvio! I was expressing myself!

SILVIO: Words! Empty, lying, treacherous words! Whore! Strumpet! Lecherous lynx and jabbering jade! You have promised yourself to another!

CLARICE: No, no, never, I swear, I would rather die alone locked up in a convent than give myself to anyone but you, my sweetest Silvio!

SILVIO: I'm not deaf, I heard Rasponi just now. You must remember your oath, and honor it!

CLARICE: Not an oath to marry him!

SILVIO: What, then?

CLARICE: Please, Silvio. I can't say.

SILVIO: Why not?

CLARICE: Because I am sworn to silence.

SILVIO: Hah—you see? Liar!

CLARICE: I'm telling the truth.

SILVIO: Then why have a secret if you've nothing to hide?

CLARICE: I have promised Federigo. Trust me.

SILVIO: You promise him, and you do not promise him? Gobbledygook!

CLARICE: I will speak simply. I love you with all my heart.

72

SILVIO: Hah! I hate you with all my soul!

CLARICE: Oh, your cruelty will kill me!

SILVIO: Better have you dead than in the arms of another!

CLARICE: That's your last word?

SILVIO: Oh, I don't know, I don't know!

CLARICE: Because it's a wish I can easily grant! *(picks up his sword, makes as if to lean upon it)*

SMERALDINA: *(rushing in)* Mistress, mistress! Have you lost your wits?! Here—give me that! *(to Silvio)* And you—you—you—man! You'd just stand there and watch her bleed to death? I suppose you think it's only your due, to have my lady eviscerate herself, as if she were to be stuffed and served up at some grisly feast? Oh! You—you—men! Please, my dear mistress, forget this—trashbag. He isn't worth your littlest fingernail! There are plenty of men around who put him in the shade, though I admit that doesn't mean much. Come—we'll put an ad in the *Gazzetto*, and by morning, you'll see, they'll all come flocking! I'll help you write it—it's always so hard to describe your own virtues and most come-hither attributes—believe me, I know, I've tried. The key is to strike the balance between modesty and truth. *(tossing sword to Silvio)* Maybe you ought to think about what she was thinking about.

CLARICE: *(weeping)* Oh! Have you no compassion, no pity? One day—no doubt after I am dead, worn to a frazzle, brokenhearted, dying of Cupid's shafts— one day you'll look back on this moment and regret, Silvio, regret with all your heart spurning and wounding your faithful and innocent Clarice! Ooooh! *(wailing, she runs off)*

SMERALDINA: Now look what you've done!

SILVIO: *I've* done!

SMERALDINA: And you just stand there, pop-eyed. I don't get it—are you in shock? Have you a drop of the milk of human kindness in your breast? You look like a spectator at a play!

SILVIO: What else? She was putting on an act! All for show! You don't think she had the slightest intention of falling on my sword, do you?

SMERALDINA: Maybe yes, maybe no. The point is, if you'd been wrong, you couldn't have fixed things. As it was, I assumed she meant to kill herself. And as it is, she's alive now, no thanks to you!

SILVIO: Women! Always exaggerating, always on the verge of hysteria!

SMERALDINA: I think it's pretty difficult to exaggerate death, don't you? Even a booby like you ought to understand that death is irrevocable.

SILVIO: What about Rasponi?

SMERALDINA: That's different, that was just misinformation, later corrected. Hah! Exaggerate! Hysterical! Yes, yes, women are always the ones, aren't we? Faithless whores, eh? But who are we unfaithful with, I'd like to know. It can't all be auto-erotic, or same sex, now, can it? Just doesn't make statistical sense. You men do what you want, we women take the rap. And why? Because you've made all the rules and passed all the laws. One day we'll get our day in court! If I were calling the shots, I'd make every man who'd broken his marriage vows carry a tree branch. What do you bet the whole town would turn into a forest? Exaggerate! Hysterical! Poo! Or ask each one to carry a thimbleful of water to the center of town—we'd have a flood in no time. Or to pick up one stone—we'd rival the great wall of China. Or . . . *(leaves)*

SILVIO: I may have lost the faithless wench! But I won't lose the chance to avenge myself on my rival! I'll split him down the middle right before her eyes! I'll force her to witness his cowardly and lingering death! I'll twist the knife, I'll slice off his head and parade it around the piazza for all to— yuch. I'm getting carried away. I'm going to be sick. *(running off)*

ACT 2

Scene 1

Brighella's inn. Truffaldino is agitated.

TRUFFALDINO: I am in deep trouble. Two masters, both late for dinner. Just you wait—they'll both stroll in at the same time and I'll have to struggle to keep up appearances, as well as wait table. Please, God, bless me now. Help me keep at least one of my jobs. Don't let me or any other of your creatures blow my cover, and I promise I'll never bother you again. Per omnia funicula funiculorum. Amen.

FLORINDO: *(entering)* Truffaldino!

TRUFFALDINO: Ah! You startled me, sir.

FLORINDO: Did you see Pasqual'?

TRUFFALDINO: We agreed I'd look for him after dinner.

FLORINDO: Right, right. But I'm so restless. I don't think I can wait that long.

TRUFFALDINO: Well, if you'd come back for dinner on time, it'd be over by now, and I could go find him. As it is . . .

FLORINDO: I know, you're right. I hope I haven't caused any inconvenience.

TRUFFALDINO: Well, as a matter of fact, you have.

FLORINDO: Impertinence!

TRUFFALDINO: You brought it up, sir, if I may say so. You ordered me to order, I ordered. Next thing I know you've left!

FLORINDO: I can't sit still, I'm—feeling very hyper.

TRUFFALDINO: Be that as it may, sir. The dinner will have been spoiled. And what about all the starving people in the American colonies and Cathay? What they wouldn't give for a nice Italian feast! But no! No, no, no, no, no! You walk out just as it's being prepared. You probably forgot about it.

FLORINDO: I did, Truffaldino, honestly. I'm upset, I'm worried, I'm suffering from excessive agitazione. *(to audience)* The truth is, I can't find out if Beatrice is here. That's all I can think about. *(to Truffaldino)* After all, dinner is just food.

TRUFFALDINO: Up to a point there, sir, I can't disagree. But food can be dreadful or sublime, and Brighella's promised us something at that upper end.

FLORINDO: *(to audience)* You think I should try the post office again? Maybe one of the gondoliers will have heard something. I can't very well go to the police station.

TRUFFALDINO: And if the pleasure of eating doesn't appeal to you sir, how about its nutritional aspects? If you don't eat, you'll get sick—especially when you're adjusting to strange surroundings. People new to Venice are prone to certain unpronounceable parasites flying through the air.

77

FLORINDO: I appreciate your concern, Truffaldino—but I really have to get some air, even if it's germ-laden. You go ahead and have dinner. Later, if I've worked up an appetite, I'll pick up something.

TRUFFALDINO: What should I tell Brighella? She's really knocked herself out putting this feast together. It was all I could do to keep from tasting a few morsels.

FLORINDO: Please, tender my apologies.

TRUFFALDINO: Ah. And how do I do that, exactly?

FLORINDO: Tell her I'm too pressed right now. *(starting out)* Oh, the money! *(removing it from his pocket)* Here's my trunk key—put this away for safekeeping. I'm so distracted with other things, I'd get my pocket picked and not even feel it. *(gives key and money to Truffaldino)*

TRUFFALDINO: *(starting out, with key)* Be right back.

FLORINDO: Later. If I'm not back by the time you've had dinner, meet me in the piazza. We'll hunt down Pasqual' together! *(leaves)*

TRUFFALDINO: Oh, Lord! I almost forgot about Pasqual'! I've got to come up with something. But, since my master said I could eat, I'll trust a good dinner to feed my invention.

BEATRICE: *(entering)* There you are!

TRUFFALDINO: I knew it!

BEATRICE: Did Signor Pantalone give you something for me?

TRUFFALDINO: For my master.

BEATRICE: Why didn't you deliver it promptly?

78

TRUFFALDINO: Uh—uh—I was on the lookout for you, so I could order dinner. I guess I forgot! Yes, yes, that's right—I forgot!

BEATRICE: I hope you haven't forgotten where you put it.

TRUFFALDINO: As a matter of fact, I have it right here.

BEATRICE: How convenient.

TRUFFALDINO: Well, since I didn't know what you wanted for dinner, I was just leaving to look for you. So I had the purse handy, in case I found you.

BEATRICE: I trust there's nothing missing.

TRUFFALDINO: *(affronted)* Are you embuing—I mean, impeaching—I mean, impugning—my honor?

BEATRICE: *(busy counting the money)* Just wondering. Idle curiosity.

TRUFFALDINO: *(to audience)* My other master seemed to think the money was his. Oh, dear, I hope he's honest. Maybe I should have two purses?

BEATRICE: Signor Pantalone will be my guest. By the looks of him, he's no gourmand. Five or six dishes ought to do—but tell Brighella to spare no expense, all right? I want to be gracious, hospitable. *(to audience)* Poor old fellow—when I saved his life I nearly gave him cardiac arrest. I need to have him on my side.

TRUFFALDINO: You'll leave it to me?

BEATRICE: To you and Brighella—she's a wonderful chef. Meanwhile, I'll fetch my guest—I hope we won't have to wait too long to eat.

TRUFFALDINO: Oh, I think this is a very efficient inn. I'm sure we'll measure up.

BEATRICE: Whoops—I almost forgot. Take this paper, please—it's a bill of exchange for forty thousand dollars. Lock it up in my trunk.

TRUFFALDINO: Right away!

BEATRICE: See you in a few minutes. *(leaves)*

TRUFFALDINO: You bet! You know, I really like serving two masters. Now I get to order another dinner. *(ringing a bell)* Signora Brighella! Signora!

BRIGHELLA: *(entering)* Signor Truffaldino! And how may I help you?

TRUFFALDINO: My master is feeling tender, and wishes to apologize, but—I no longer need that dinner for one I just ordered. *(to audience)* How I wish I could eat it myself!

BRIGHELLA: These things happen, Signor Truffaldino—think nothing of it.

TRUFFALDINO: I need another, more lavish dinner for two—my master will be having a guest. So he wants something spettacoloso, yet semplice, elegante, di buon gusto!

BRIGHELLA: Qualcosa superbo, magnifico! Two persons, four courses. We will start with bagna cauda.

TRUFFALDINO: No, no, my master doesn't want a warm bath, he wants dinner. Later the bath. Maybe a massage. . . .

BRIGHELLA: My dear Signor Truffaldino, I understand that your master wants his dinner. Bagna cauda is a warm sauce for vegetables—a little cream, garlic, anchovies, and a fine white truffle shaved into the sauce. A bit of bread, sweet pepper strips, fennel stalks—um! Perfetto!

TRUFFALDINO: That does sound good—and then?

BRIGHELLA: A small dish on the side, perhaps—funghi marinati—with the finest extra virgin olive oil just penetrating the mushrooms—

TRUFFALDINO: That sounds backwards.

BRIGHELLA: —delizioso!

TRUFFALDINO: Umhm! And then?

BRIGHELLA: A zuppa di pesce, perhaps—we will be inspired by the catch of the day. Or a frittata alla Sardegnola—no, no—too ordinary.

TRUFFALDINO: Sounds good to me.

BRIGHELLA: Then I'll make one for you later. Then . . . let's see . . . a risotto Milanese—that's with a hint of saffron—peas with a bit of prosciutto—perhaps a veal scaloppine al limone—and then, for dessert . . . what?

TRUFFALDINO: Gelati—various—pistachio, vanilla, coffee, cherry Garcia!

BRIGHELLA: No, no, something lighter—my baked peaches, perhaps.

TRUFFALDINO: I loooove peaches!

BRIGHELLA: Well, you'll really love them after you've had one of mine.

TRUFFALDINO: I'll bet I will.

BRIGHELLA: I blanch them, peel the skins, remove the pits, and scoop out the flesh.

TRUFFALDINO: Oh, it sounds sublime!

BRIGHELLA: Each peach half now has a deep space in its center.

TRUFFALDINO: Better and better.

BRIGHELLA: So I mix the pulp with crushed almond macaroons, stuff the halves—

TRUFFALDINO: UMMMMM.

BRIGHELLA: Arrange them side by side—

TRUFFALDINO: Oh, yes!

BRIGHELLA: —on a baking dish, and baste them with a bit of sugar syrup as they bake!

TRUFFALDINO: O, paradiso! Molto aromatico, piacevole, gustoso! *(about to expire)*

BRIGHELLA: Signor Truffaldino—are you all right?

TRUFFALDINO: Oh, I am beside myself with your descriptions, Signorina. However! Duty calls! *(abruptly pulling himself together)* You may be the culinary expert, but I am the best table-layer, waiter, and busboy in the business. So allow me to arrange the table. Otherwise, my master may think I'm dispensable. Hmmm . . . let me see, let me see. *(laying an imaginary table, he tears off bits of the bill of exchange to illustrate placement)* The bagna cauda, the zuppa, the funghi, the risotto, the frittata—

BRIGHELLA: No frittata.

TRUFFALDINO: I forgot! *(wads up "frittata" paper, tosses it away.)* Now, the peaches . . . hmm . . . I'm stumped!

BRIGHELLA: We'll clear the table completely *(sweeping away the bits of paper)* and then serve the peaches!

TRUFFALDINO: Wait a minute, wait a minute, I wasn't finished! *(retrieving the papers)* See what you've done? Now we'll have to start over! *(tearing up more of the bill of exchange)*

82

BRIGHELLA: It's just as well—I was going to suggest another arrangement. *(tearing off her own bits of paper)* And you forgot the scaloppine al limone!

TRUFFALDINO: I did? So I did. *(tears off a "scaloppine" bit)* Please—let me do it. The bagna, the zuppa, the funghi, the risotto, the scaloppine al limone—perfetto!

BRIGHELLA: You forgot my peaches.

TRUFFALDINO: Never—your peaches are unforgettable. I liked your idea—we'll just clear the whole table *(sweeping away yet another pile of papers)* making a tavola rasa—and set your peaches smack dab in the middle—the pièce de resistance!

(Beatrice and Pantalone enter, take in the blizzard)

BEATRICE: Well! What's going on here?

TRUFFALDINO: Master! We were just putting the fine points on the place settings.

BEATRICE: And what's all this paper?

TRUFFALDINO: Uh-oh—the paper he told me to lock safely away!

BEATRICE: I don't believe it—that's my bill of exchange—you've just torn up forty thousand dollars!

PANTALONE: What? Well! So he has, so he has. *(to audience)* I wonder if I could pull a fast one here—he might see through me.

TRUFFALDINO: *(scrambling to pick up the papers)* Uh—no harm done, Master—I'll just stick them back together again. Brighella—do you have a bit of bread?

BEATRICE: Bonehead! I never know what you'll do next! I've half a mind to give you a good thrashing.

TRUFFALDINO: Please, Master—they don't allow that sort of thing here—do they, Signor Pantalone?

PANTALONE: Oh, they do, but only when it's warranted.

BEATRICE: Don't you think this is pure folly?

PANTALONE: Uh, actually, Signor Rasponi, I can write out another bill—no harm done, none at all. *(to audience)* Plenty of time to cheat him after he's tied the knot.

BEATRICE: Well, thank you. But what if the bill had been written in some far-off place? Honestly, Truffaldino!

TRUFFALDINO: Master, I am sorry if I have caused you some inconvenience—

BEATRICE: I'll say!

TRUFFALDINO: But it's only because Brighella doesn't know how to set a proper table.

BRIGHELLA: I like that.

TRUFFALDINO: Though to give her her due, she is a great cook. And I am a perfectionist when it comes to laying a table—or anything else, for that matter—serving, waiting, presenting, and so on, ad infinitum, etcetera. These are the crafts of my calling—and I defer to no one when it comes to—

BEATRICE: Truffaldino!

TRUFFALDINO: Yes?

84

BEATRICE: Stop talking, and move along. Brighella, is our dinner ready?

BRIGHELLA: Well, Signor Rasponi, I'll need a few more minutes—after all, with four courses . . .

BEATRICE: Four!

PANTALONE: No, please, something simple—risotto, some soup.

BRIGHELLA: My scallopine al limone, Signor Pantalone—oh! You must try my scallopine al limone! I would never recover if you rejected my—

PANTALONE: Actually, Brighella—this is a bit embarrassing—but I've had a few root canals lately—

BRIGHELLA: Oooh!

PANTALONE: Yes, I know, hurts just to say it. So—something soft—meatballs, rice balls, matzoh balls. Nothing periodontally challenging. Something I can mash.

BRIGHELLA: Leave it to me, Signor. Meanwhile, if you'll go in? *(gesturing them into a private room at one side)*

PANTALONE: *(leaving)* Well, my dear near son-in-law, you are most hospitable.

BEATRICE: *(leaving)* Oh, it's nothing, really. *(to Truffaldino)* Less entertainment, more utility.

TRUFFALDINO: Well! I like that! As if I didn't know my place! Entertainment? What does he mean?

(Pandora enters, carrying wine into the room. Nora follows with a tureen of soup.)

TRUFFALDINO: Uh-hm! That smells delicious. Excuse me—

NORA: Sir?

TRUFFALDINO: My master likes me to verify the blend of seasonings, the freshness of ingredients, the perfection of the technique.

NORA: Really, sir—we know what we are doing.

TRUFFALDINO: Ah, but can you be sure? All we can really know is that we are here.

NORA: Please, sir, they are waiting.

TRUFFALDINO: No, no, we are waiting, my good woman. Now *(fishing a spoon from his pocket)*—just a wee taste to—hmhmhm! Perfetto! *(pocketing spoon)*

(Pandora returns to the kitchen)

NORA: You're sure you're finished—there's plenty where that came from.

TRUFFALDINO: No, no, there are many dishes—I must keep my tastebuds at the ready. *(taking tureen)* Though if you had a morsel of bread so I could clean my palate . . .

NORA: *(returning to kitchen)* The airs these northerners put on!

PANDORA: *(entering with a platter)* Where is that fellow? I don't mind doing the wine service, but—

TRUFFALDINO: *(entering)* Ah! The aroma calls! Wafting from—what, exactly?

PANDORA: *(handing him the platter)* The bagna cauda— I don't suppose you even know what that is up in Bergamo.

TRUFFALDINO: Au contraire, mon ami. It's—it's—not worth mentioning.

PANDORA: Hah! *(returns to kitchen)*

86

TRUFFALDINO: *(inhaling its aroma)* Ooh! But these vegetables are so perfectly arranged—maybe if I just *(dipping his finger into the sauce)*—ever so delicately. Umhm. *(squinting at the level of the sauce)* They'll never miss it. In fact . . . *(dipping another finger)* I wonder . . . *(tasting)* if it needs just a soupçon of garlic. These tantalizing tastes are too small to tell. *(getting spoon, about to dig in)*

FLORINDO: *(entering)* Truffaldino!

TRUFFALDINO: Agh! Sir!

FLORINDO: What are you doing?

TRUFFALDINO: Quality control, sir—I always check the food when I'm serving in a new place.

FLORINDO: You're serving my dinner before I arrive?

TRUFFALDINO: Well, sir—I thought if I got started, somehow, perchance, you'd appear.

FLORINDO: That's ridiculous.

TRUFFALDINO: But it worked.

FLORINDO: Well, I never begin with vegetables—I much prefer soup. So, if you don't mind . . .

TRUFFALDINO: Whatever you wish, sir. Although here in Venice, they take soup last. *(moves slowly toward kitchen)*

FLORINDO: Get a move on—after dinner I'll need a nap before we meet Pasqual'.

TRUFFALDINO: *(wincing at the name)* Uh, yes, sir.

FLORINDO: Our best, last hope! *(goes into a room apart)*

TRUFFALDINO: Right away, sir. *(walking in place)* Quick as a wink.

(Now that Florindo is out of sight, Truffaldino dashes into Beatrice's room with the bagna cauda. Nora enters with a dish of mushrooms.)

FLORINDO: *(calling)* Truffaldino! I am waiting!

TRUFFALDINO: *(dashing back with the soup tureen, he thrusts it at Nora)* Coming, sir. Here—take this.

NORA: *(of her dish)* After you take this.

(They try various ways of handing off the two dishes at once. Finally Truffaldino takes the dish on the crook of his elbow as he hands the tureen to Nora.)

FLORINDO: Truffaldino!

TRUFFALDINO: On my way, sir! Where there's a will . . .

NORA: You are too much.

TRUFFALDINO: Why, thank you. If you could top off the soup a little, and set a place for the gentleman in the next room, I'll owe you one. *(Nora flounces off with the soup)* Hmm—this must be the extra virgin olive oil right here, penetrating the . . . hmhmhm! *(takes it to Beatrice)*

(Nora returns with a place setting, goes into Florindo's room.)

TRUFFALDINO: *(catching sight of her as he returns)* Good work!

NORA: *(returning to kitchen)* All set.

TRUFFALDINO: The soup, the soup!

PANDORA: *(entering with the soup)* Maybe we should just take care of the gentleman, so you can look after your own—

TRUFFALDINO: No, no—I do upfront. You do backup.

PANDORA & NORA: We always do backup.

(they sing some doo-wop, Truffaldino doing the main vocal)

TRUFFALDINO: *(of the soup)* Allow me. And get the scallopine al limone! *(goes into Florindo's room)*

BEATRICE: *(calling)* Truffaldino!

NORA: Without us, he's nothing.

PANDORA: I say, let's ditch him.

NORA: We still get our tips.

PANDORA: He's just an egomaniac.

BEATRICE: Truffaldino!

(he enters carrying tureen)

NORA: Your master's calling. *(returning to kitchen)*

TRUFFALDINO: Which—oh, yes, right. *(calling)* Coming, sir. *(thrusting tureen at Pandora)* You mind? *(going to Beatrice)*

PANDORA: *(returning to kitchen with tureen)* What's the difference?

NORA: *(with scallopine for Florindo)* You think I should just serve this?

(Pandora shrugs, goes into kitchen. Truffaldino returns with plates from Beatrice's room.)

FLORINDO: *(calling)* Truffaldino!

TRUFFALDINO: Here—I'll trade.

NORA: Isn't it easier if I just—

TRUFFALDINO: No, it's not, please, trust me.

NORA: I want to serve this!

TRUFFALDINO: Well, so do I!

NORA: It's my job!

TRUFFALDINO: No, it's mine!

FLORINDO: Truffaldino!

TRUFFALDINO: Hear that? Is he calling Nora or Pandora? *(snatches the dish, goes to Florindo)* No, he's calling—

BEATRICE: Truffaldino!

NORA: Well! He just wants to do it all! Where does that leave me? Out of a job!

PANDORA: *(returning with platter of meatballs)* Who gets these?

NORA: Search me. Signor Know-It-All will tell you, I'm sure.

PANDORA: I don't want to ask him—he's already too big for his breeches.

NORA: Well, I don't want to ask him! He's so conceited he makes me sick!

TRUFFALDINO: *(returning with Florindo's dirty dishes)* Well—taking a little break, hm?

NORA: *(to Pandora)* See what I mean? *(to Truffaldino)* Why don't I help you out and take those gross plates off your pampered hands?

TRUFFALDINO: *(giving her the plates)* You're sweet. Thanks.

NORA: Oh, do not mention it, charmed and all that, I am sure. *(setting plates down)* That's as far as I go. *(flounces out)*

PANDORA: Since your hands are free, you can serve these. *(thrusts them at him)*

TRUFFALDINO: *(taking the platter)* What are these? And who are they for?

PANDORA: *(flouncing out)* Up to you, Signor Bigshot!

TRUFFALDINO: I think I've met my Waterloo. And I'm sure I'd remember if we'd talked meatballs—meatballs I know. None of this soup of the day and Al Capone—I mean, al limone. Just good old meatballs. These couldn't be the funghi marinata, now, could they? I can't really have a bite—they'd notice. If I ask Brighella, she'll smell something fishy—hey, is it the—no, that's liquid, and I served it already. If I serve it to the wrong master, well, eventually these acorns become mighty oaks, I can tell you. *(spies dirty plates)* That's it! *(sets down platter, rubs two plates clean on this apron, divides the meatballs, dribbles gravy over them with a flourish)* But there's an odd number—I can't cut it in half . . . nothing for it. *(pops meatball into his mouth, chews with delight, swallows, beams)* Have to treat them as equals, you know. Strict justice! By the book! *(goes to Beatrice with one plate)*

(Brighella comes in, peaches aloft)

BRIGHELLA: *(calling)* Truffaldino!

TRUFFALDINO: *(returning, picking up the second plate of meatballs)* Signora. *(starting toward Florindo's room)*

BRIGHELLA: No, no, no, the meatballs are for Signor Pantalone.

TRUFFALDINO: Uh, yes, that's right. But he's sending these to the other gentleman with his compliments. *(dashing out)*

91

BRIGHELLA: *(to audience)* Well, if they're acquainted, why didn't they eat together, and save us some trouble?

TRUFFALDINO: *(returning)* And may I say, Signora Brighella, you have outdone yourself!

BRIGHELLA: Really?

TRUFFALDINO: Really.

BRIGHELLA: Wait till they taste my peaches!

TRUFFALDINO: Ah, those peaches! I almost forgot!

BRIGHELLA: *(handing him the dish)* I have to check on the coffee. *(leaves)*

TRUFFALDINO: *(of the peaches)* They're just as she said. Round in shape, and firm in flesh, and fully packed—hmhm! You really think they need this, after all the dishes they've had? I'm sure neither of my masters would mind if I had just a little bitty taste—maybe from the underside, just to be safe. *(getting his spoon, he shaves off a bit)* Oh, that's good—the almond is just right! One more, and then I'm back on track. *(shaves off another bit)* Oh! Un-believable! Maybe they don't even want dessert. *(digging into the dish)*

BEATRICE: *(calling)* Truffaldino!

TRUFFALDINO: *(calling)* Coming!

FLORINDO: Truffaldino!

TRUFFALDINO: Coming!

NORA: *(entering with a tray)* The coffee.

TRUFFALDINO: Thanks! *(dashes to Beatrice)*

PANDORA: *(entering as Truffaldino returns)* The cheese.

TRUFFALDINO: Thanks. *(dashes to Florindo, returns)*

NORA & PANDORA: Will there be anything else, sir?

TRUFFALDINO: Well, as a matter of fact, no. *(of Florindo)* He wants a nap. *(of Beatrice)* And he's doing business, doesn't want to be disturbed. And now you can wait on me!

NORA & PANDORA: Hah!

TRUFFALDINO: I'll make it worth your while, ladies. *(to audience)* After all, I'm on double wages. *(to Nora and Pandora)* And I'm not fussy—I'll take potluck!

(Nora & Pandora flounce out)

Well. That's not very nice. Venetians! *(picks up what is left of the dish of peaches)* I'll just finish this up and work backwards! *(eating)* Umhmumhm! After all, in Venice they eat the soup last! I've never felt better in my life! Double your masters, double your fun—I don't know why I didn't think of this a lot earlier! And there's lots more where this came from! *(exits to the kitchen)*

(Smeraldina enters, playing directly to the audience)

SMERALDINA: Honestly! First my mistress can hardly wait to commit suicide because she cannot marry Silvio. Then she nearly has a fit because I don't drop everything I'm doing—for her, I should point out—and spring over here to deliver a letter to the other guy, who, as we all know—but I am sworn to secrecy! Well, it's not for us maids to reason why. But when the person you're working for acts crazy, you begin to feel a little crazy yourself. *(calling)* Hello—buon giorno! Anybody here?

(Pandora & Nora appear)

Well—very efficient!

PANDORA & NORA: Welcome to the Inn of the Dove, Brighella of Bergamo, Proprieteressa. How may we help you?

SMERALDINA: I have a letter for Signor Federigo Rasponi.

PANDORA: *(gesturing to Beatrice's room)* He's just finished dinner.

SMERALDINA: Thank you. *(starting out)*

NORA: No, no—in that room. *(gesturing to Florindo's room)*

SMERALDINA: *(changing course)* Thank you again.

PANDORA: Please. It's this room.

SMERALDINA: *(another about face)* If you're sure. *(starting out)*

PANDORA: Sure I'm sure—he's with Signor Pantalone dei Bisognosi!

SMERALDINA: *(halting in her tracks)* My master! *(to Pandora)* Uh—actually—is Signor Rasponi's servant around? I'd just as soon deliver the letter to him.

NORA: Now you tell us!

PANDORA: We get it. Un momento.

NORA & PANDORA: Sisterhood is powerful! *(they leave)*

SMERALDINA: If my master comes out, I'll—say I'm looking for him. Good. Only . . . why am I looking for him? Oh! Intrigue's not in my job description! *(Truffaldino enters, still wearing his dinner napkin, much sauced, and pouring himself a glass of wine. Concentrating on this task, he does not immediately see Smeraldina.)* As cute as ever!

94

TRUFFALDINO: Somebody wants to see me?

SMERALDINA: I hope I'm not interrupting anything.

TRUFFALDINO: Signorina Smeraldina! What an unexpected pleasure! Now that I'm just finishing my dinner, I can't think of anything I'd rather do than gaze into your sparkling eyes! To your health! *(drinks)*

SMERALDINA: *(to audience)* Oh! He pushes all my buttons! *(to Truffaldino)* I don't want to take you from your dinner.

TRUFFALDINO: *(setting down wine, untying napkin)* Oh, I was nearly finished. Just let me make myself a bit more presentable—I didn't know I'd be meeting a lady.

SMERALDINA: *(to audience)* A lady! *(pulling herself together)* Well, sir, my mistress has sent this letter to Signor Rasponi. I wonder if you would mind delivering it for me.

TRUFFALDINO: I would consider it an honor to perform even the most trifling service for you, Signorina.

SMERALDINA: *(to audience)* See what I mean?

TRUFFALDINO: But first I have a message myself.

SMERALDINA: You do? Fancy that!

TRUFFALDINO: *(to audience)* I fancy her.

SMERALDINA: And who has given you this message?

TRUFFALDINO: Oh, a man of unquestioned honesty. Have you heard of Truffaldin' Battocchio?

SMERALDINA: Sounds familiar. I'm not sure I've met him. *(to audience)* Isn't that his name?

TRUFFALDINO: A modest fellow. Dark, in a sultry Mediterranean way. Not too hairy, not too smooth. Well proportioned, as Leonardo would have drawn him. Has the softest, velvetiest, smolderingest eyes in all of Venice.

SMERALDINA: Ah—I'm sure I've never met him.

TRUFFALDINO: Is an excellent factotum, a genuine jack-of-all-trades—butler, valet, waiter, maitre d', porter, messenger, and general handyman.

SMERALDINA: Is he twins?

TRUFFALDINO: Only one Truffaldin' Battocchio— though he does, on occasion, do double duty. Most important of all, he is head-over-heels in love with you!

SMERALDINA: Sir! Do not mock me!

TRUFFALDINO: The problem is, he is extremely shy. And he hates it when women turn him down.

SMERALDINA: *(offended)* Oh? A frequent occurrence?

TRUFFALDINO: He has suffered a broken heart once or twice—no more than most men his age.

SMERALDINA: Hmph!

TRUFFALDINO: But this time he just knows it's the real thing! If you gave even the slightest hint that you might—entertain the tiniest possibility of returning even . . . just an in-fi-ni-te-si-mal morsel of his affection—why, he would trample his shyness into the dust, grind it to smithereens, and present himself.

SMERALDINA: *(to audience)* What should I do? *(to Truffaldino)* Well, sir, assuming that this man is as sincere as you say—

96

TRUFFALDINO: He is the soul of sincerity, the essence of earnestness! He really, really means it!

SMERALDINA: Well, then . . . I might possibly entertain the tiniest possibility of returning just a small morsel of his affection.

TRUFFALDINO: Would you like to meet him now?

SMERALDINA: Maybe see him from afar—no chemistry, no meeting.

TRUFFALDINO: One second. *(dashes off)*

SMERALDINA: *(crushed)* I guess I was wrong. *(Truffaldino reenters dashingly, takes her in his arms, and leads her in a tango, ending with a dip and a spin. Still the gallant, he dashes off.)* Oooh, woo, woo, woo, woo, woo, woo! I feel like a little kid.

TRUFFALDINO: *(reentering)* Well? Any chemistry?

SMERALDINA: But—that was you!

TRUFFALDINO: Right!

SMERALDINA: Why didn't you just come out with it.

TRUFFALDINO: I told you, he's—I'm—we're—shy.

SMERALDINA: *(to audience)* I am melting.

TRUFFALDINO: Please, I'm dying to have some kind of answer.

SMERALDINA: Well, I . . .

TRUFFALDINO: Hurry up, hurry up, the suspense!! *(cringing)*

SMERALDINA: I'm shy myself.

TRUFFALDINO: So we've got that in common.

SMERALDINA: And we're both servants.

TRUFFALDINO: So there wouldn't be any social ladder to climb or descend.

SMERALDINA: And there is something about you . . .

TRUFFALDINO: Same to you, same to you. Oh, and I assume you're a virgin.

SMERALDINA: You have to ask?

TRUFFALDINO: Darn!

SMERALDINA: I mean, isn't it obvious?

TRUFFALDINO: Well, when you put it that way . . . I'm—not married either.

SMERALDINA: I should hope not. *(to audience)* Notice how he puts it—good old double standard.

TRUFFALDINO: Speaking of hope—may I have any?

SMERALDINA: Up till now, I've never found a man I really felt attracted to.

TRUFFALDINO: Ah—animal magnetism.

SMERALDINA: I guess. Believe me, plenty of men approached me, but I never felt the right—fluster.

TRUFFALDINO: A sort of tingling all over?

SMERALDINA: Yes, a sort of—shudder.

TRUFFALDINO: And while you're shuddering, you can't stop grinning.

SMERALDINA: That's it—exactly it! I'd better stop there, before I go too far.

TRUFFALDINO: No, please—would you marry me? I'm on pins and needles to get a straight answer.

SMERALDINA: Please—after you take the letter.

TRUFFALDINO: The letter! You see? You dazzle me so, I forget my duty. What's in it?

SMERALDINA: No idea—how I wish I knew!

TRUFFALDINO: I can't take it unless I know what's in it. I don't want to risk bearing bad news.

SMERALDINA: Well, I can't take it—my master's in there with your master—he always blames me if my mistress does something he doesn't like.

TRUFFALDINO: I guess we have to open it.

SMERALDINA: They'll know!

TRUFFALDINO: Leave it to me, sweetheart—sealing letters is one of my skills.

SMERALDINA: Great—no problem.

TRUFFALDINO: I assume you can read.

SMERALDINA: I'm a little out of practice—but I'll bet you can read like a scholar!

TRUFFALDINO: Oh, I'm a little out of practice, too— what with all my factotum work, there's not much time left for reading. *(opens letter, hands it to her)* Read away!

SMERALDINA: *(handing it back)* After you.

TRUFFALDINO: *(handing it back)* Please—you know your lady's handwriting.

SMERALDINA: *(trying)* Just a lot of scribbling.

TRUFFALDINO: *(checking)* I'll say. Wait—I think that's an—an "m."

SMERALDINA: That?! It's an "r"!

TRUFFALDINO: Yes, well, they have a lot in common, the "m" and the "r." "Marinara" and "ricotta," for instance. "Mozzarella" and "ravioli." *(of her)* "Modest" and "ravishing."

SMERALDINA: *(poring over the letter)* I think that's a—

TRUFFALDINO: *(poring over her)* An "i"—there's a dot, see?

(Beatrice and Pantalone enter)

SMERALDINA: Isn't that a full stop?

PANTALONE: What are you doing here?

SMERALDINA: Uh, nothing, sir, I came to look for you.

PANTALONE: So?? Here I am.

SMERALDINA: My mistress, sir, she . . . uh . . . she . . .

BEATRICE: Another letter?

TRUFFALDINO: Uh, well, sort of—uh—

BEATRICE: *(snatching it)* Addressed to me! This is becoming a bad habit! Look here, Signor Pantalone—a letter from your daughter. Silvio—insanely jealous—and this impertinent riffraff has the temerity to open it!

PANTALONE: *(to Smeraldina)* And you conspired with him?

SMERALDINA: I am innocent as a flower in May!

BEATRICE: Confess! Who opened this?

TRUFFALDINO: Not I.

SMERALDINA: Not I.

PANTALONE: How did it get here?

SMERALDINA: Truffaldino was bringing it to his master.

TRUFFALDINO: And Smeraldina brought it to Truffaldino.

SMERALDINA: Some hero!

PANTALONE: So it's your fault! I should give you a slap.

SMERALDINA: You do, you'll regret it.

PANTALONE: Flippant jade!

SMERALDINA: Watch your heart, now. If you chase me, you'll kill yourself. *(dashing off)*

PANTALONE: Impertinent minx! *(hurrying after her)*

TRUFFALDINO: And who's left to fend for himself?

BEATRICE: *(reviewing the letter)* Poor Clarice! She is at her wit's end! Maybe I should spill the beans—otherwise, who knows what she might do? *(Truffaldino starts to sneak off)* Going somewhere?

TRUFFALDINO: Of course not. They also serve who only stand and wait.

BEATRICE: Because I think you've got something coming. Two letters in one day!

TRUFFALDINO: Please, sir, have mercy!

BEATRICE: I'll be lenient this time. . . . *(taking Truffaldino's stick)* But not as lenient as last time! *(to audience)* This hurts me more than it hurts him— but I have to do it like a man. *(with her back to the inn, she beats him)*

TRUFFALDINO: Mercy, mercy!

FLORINDO: *(at the window above)* What?! What's this? *(starts down)*

BEATRICE: That should teach you! When I get back, I want my trunk unpacked! *(discards stick, leaves)*

TRUFFALDINO: Oh, sir! Oh! I ache all over! I'd rather be fired than beaten! Oh! Have I no recourse? Does Venice have an occupational safety and health administration? A servants' abuse hotline?

FLORINDO: *(entering)* What's going on? I need my rest, I can't think straight!

TRUFFALDINO: Oh, sir—I've been beaten!

FLORINDO: But why?

TRUFFALDINO: An accident! A misunderstanding! I—uh—was clearing my throat, and my—projectile misfired on his—shoe!

FLORINDO: And you just let it happen! Without fighting back? Don't you know a servant's behavior reflects upon his master? Coward! Weasel! *(picking up stick)* You'll have to toughen up if you're going to serve me! *(beating him)* How's that?

TRUFFALDINO: Oh, sir, please! Please, you don't understand!

FLORINDO: I don't, eh? Well, maybe you'll explain it to me later. And get my clothes aired. *(throws down stick, leaves)*

TRUFFALDINO: Oh! Oh, oh, oh, my aching butt! But! I have earned twice my usual salary! *(moaning and limping)* Oooh. When you're twice as busy, you can't let the pain of two beatings distract you. Because if you did, you'd never get anything done! Which one wants his clothes aired? *(calling)* Nora! Pandora! I need a little help getting my masters' trunks in here, so I can give their clothes a good airing.

PANDORA: *(entering)* Your master has two trunks?

TRUFFALDINO: One. But I have two.

NORA: *(entering)* Trunks? So there's three?

TRUFFALDINO: Let's start over. There's one of each of us—

PANDORA: That's three.

TRUFFALDINO: There's one of each of my masters.

NORA: That's—

TRUFFALDINO: Two. And each one has one trunk. Get it?

NORA: We figured that out at dinner.

PANDORA: You think we're stupid?

TRUFFALDINO: I think you're both beautiful—

NORA: Well!

PANDORA: Idiot!

TRUFFALDINO: And I think you'd like to help me—

PANDORA: Hah!

TRUFFALDINO: If I pay you handsomely. *(running what follows all together)* But if we don't get started pretty soon and forget the arithmetic lesson, one master'll be back or the other master'll wake up and the clothes won't have been freshened up in the fresh Venetian air and I'll be in for another couple of beatings, so could you please move it! *(realizing he is shouting, suddenly lowering his voice)* Quiet!—he's asleep.

NORA: *(to Pandora)* I do one, you do one. *(goes out with Truffaldino)*

PANDORA: Did you ever hear of a servant with two masters? There's something going on here—I wonder if he's a thief. Hauling two trunks!

(Nora and Truffaldino tiptoe in and carefully set down the trunk. Truffaldino signals to Pandora, who follows him into Beatrice's room.)

NORA: I wonder if Signora Brighella knows he's got two masters? She told me he was serving Signor Federigo, not—

(Truffaldino tiptoes in with Pandora, carrying the other trunk)

PANDORA: Over here?

TRUFFALDINO: Fine, fine. *(they set down the trunk)* Thanks very much. *(they flounce out)*

I wonder which key . . . *(tries to figure out which is which, gives up, takes a stab, proves right)* There—if I'm not clever, sometimes I'm lucky! And this other one must *(opens second trunk)*—aha! Now, let's just get these things out of their stifling prison. . . . *(hanging clothes on hooks)* Always check your pockets, my mother used to say—sometimes I'd forget about a hidden sweet, and then it'd all come out in the wash! *(finding something in Beatrice's suit)* See? *(taking out a portrait)* Well, isn't he handsome—and familiar! Let's see—whose suit is this, anyway? The one who looks like this fellow? Or the one who doesn't? And is this just another coincidence on the road of life, or—

FLORINDO: *(calling from his room)* Truffaldino!

TRUFFALDINO: Did I say lucky? *(panicked, he starts repacking the trunks)* Please, God, one more time, it really is the last, I promise. I know I promised before, but—

FLORINDO: Truffaldino! Are you deaf?

TRUFFALDINO: *(to audience)* I have a ringing in my ears since that beating, not that he cares. *(calling)* Coming, coming! *(repacking)* This suit was in this trunk, right? And these papers—uh . . .

FLORINDO: *(calling)* I'm waiting!

TRUFFALDINO: Yes, sir, yes! *(stuffs everything in helter-skelter)* Coming, coming, coming, sir, one more minute, I'm on my way, be right there, the check is in the mail, I'm just about—

FLORINDO: *(entering in his shirtsleeves)* Truffaldino! *(Truffaldino freezes)* Are my clothes ready?

TRUFFALDINO: Just about, sir.

FLORINDO: And this other trunk?

TRUFFALDINO: Other trunk? What oth— Oh! There's another trunk, isn't there. Well, well, well—I guess that's reasonable, I mean, we're in an inn, travelers stop here, they often have trunks, so . . . No idea, sir, not a clue.

FLORINDO: Unpack my coat.

TRUFFALDINO: You got it! *(getting it from the trunk, humming or whistling, he helps Florindo out of his dressing gown and into the coat)*

FLORINDO: I'm restless, it's nippy. I need fresh air to think straight.

TRUFFALDINO: Oh, sir—it does become you!

FLORINDO: *(finding portrait in his pocket)* What's this?

TRUFFALDINO: *(to audience)* Oh, dear—if he doesn't know, it's not his.

FLORINDO: *(to audience)* My own portrait—that I gave to Beatrice! *(to Truffaldino)* How did this get into my pocket?

TRUFFALDINO: *(to audience)* Why do I have to have all the answers? I'd like to ask a few questions once in a while. *(to Florindo)* Well, sir, that portrait belongs to me.

FLORINDO: What?

TRUFFALDINO: Yes, yes, to me it belongs. *(to audience)* My lies don't sound right even to me. *(to Florindo)* A former master left it to me.

FLORINDO: No.

TRUFFALDINO: Oh yes, sir, he did. He left me a few other things, which I sold. *(suddenly pious)* I kept this because—because it reminded me of you, sir.

FLORINDO: How long ago did your master die?

TRUFFALDINO: Uh—about a week ago, I think. I can't remember—I was in denial. Just before I met you. I think. As I say, I was—

FLORINDO: Basta! What was your master's name?

TRUFFALDINO: Uh—he traveled incognito.

FLORINDO: How long did you serve him?

TRUFFALDINO: *(to audience)* Damn these questions! *(to Florindo)* Only a few . . . days, sir.

FLORINDO: *(to audience)* Worse and worse! He must have been Beatrice! Oh, I am distraught! *(to Truffaldino)* Was he young, clean shaven?

TRUFFALDINO: Uh . . . yes and . . . yes.

FLORINDO: *(with a great sigh)* My heart is breaking.

TRUFFALDINO: *(to audience)* This seems to be working. As long as I don't get another beating. . . .

FLORINDO: Was he from Turin, by any chance?

TRUFFALDINO: The very place!

FLORINDO: Every syllable twists the knife! Dead! Only the good die young!

TRUFFALDINO: And clean shaven, sir. A terrible accident of some kind, don't know what kind. *(to audience)* A detail or two—but not too many.

FLORINDO: Buried here?

TRUFFALDINO: *(to audience)* Whoops! *(to Florindo)* Uh, not here, sir. As a matter of fact, not buried.

FLORINDO: Desecrated!

TRUFFALDINO: Another servant had him mailed home in a coffin.

FLORINDO: That same servant who got you to go to the post?

TRUFFALDINO: Very good, sir, Pasqual', exactly!

FLORINDO: Proof positive! Oh! I—oh! *(goes into his room, flings himself down)*

TRUFFALDINO: Oh, well—I'm sorry he's taking it so hard. Could it be his own brother? Oh, dear—I've got to clear this up before the other one . . . uh-oh. This reminds me of some play by Shakespeare I saw at the Bergamo fair last summer.

BEATRICE: *(entering with Pantalone)* I am positive the last consignment has been listed twice.

PANTALONE: Possible, possible. Of course, if we have overcharged you, we will make good on our mistake.

BEATRICE: I have my own copy of the list. Truffaldino, fetch my trunk key. Why is my trunk in here?

TRUFFALDINO: *(handing her the key)* I've just aired your clothes, sir.

BEATRICE: Whose trunk is that?

TRUFFALDINO: Another traveler, just arrived.

BEATRICE: My memorandum book.

TRUFFALDINO: Yes, sir. *(praying)* Just this once—I forgot for a second I had two masters. *(opens trunk, rummages for book)*

PANTALONE: You can't get good help these days. Even the simplest accounting—

TRUFFALDINO: This? *(handing it to Beatrice)*

BEATRICE: *(taking it absently)* We'll settle it in a—this isn't mine!

(Truffaldino just rolls his eyes, or otherwise lets us know he's in hot water)

(to audience) Letters that I wrote to Florindo! His accounts! Oh!

PANTALONE: Sir! Are you all right?

BEATRICE: A mere bagatelle. *(to Truffaldino)* How did this book get into my trunk? The truth!

TRUFFALDINO: It's mine, sir, and I put it there to keep it out of the hands of thieves and brigands! *(to audience)* It worked once, why not twice?

BEATRICE: And you didn't notice you were giving me your own book?

TRUFFALDINO: *(to audience)* He is quick. *(to Beatrice)* Well, sir, I was rushing, you were in a hurry, I didn't notice.

BEATRICE: And how did you get this book?

TRUFFALDINO: Another master, here in Venice, died a few days ago, left it to me.

BEATRICE: But I met you in Verona.

TRUFFALDINO: I'd just come from Venice.

BEATRICE: Oh, be still, my heart! Was his name— Florindo?

TRUFFALDINO: Florindo, yes, Florindo, now that you mention it, it was definitely—

BEATRICE: Aretusi?

TRUFFALDINO: A-re-tu-si? Sounds right, sounds right— it was Aretusi!

BEATRICE: How did he die? Where is he buried?

TRUFFALDINO: He fell into the canal and drowned. His body was never recovered!

BEATRICE: Oh! And I shall never recover!

PANTALONE: Please, sir, sit down—air, air!

(Truffaldino fans Beatrice as Pantalone pours a glass of water)

BEATRICE: What's the point? Florindo dead! All my stratagems for naught!

PANTALONE: *(offering the glass of water)* Drink this.

BEATRICE: *(waving it away)* I set out in the dead of night, dressed as a man, abandoning my relatives, confronting danger, enduring peril, all, all for Florindo! And Florindo is dead!

TRUFFALDINO: They do take my tales very hard, don't they?

BEATRICE: Bad enough I lost my brother—but my lover, too! Oh, oh, oh! These ridiculous trousers— pointless! Dearest beloved, soul of my soul, light of my life! I must bury myself in grief! I will walk in your wake to the grave! *(goes into her room)*

PANTALONE: Did you hear that?

TRUFFALDINO: I did, sir. It reminds me of a play I saw, Romeo e Giulietta, at the Bergamo fair. They were from Verona, I think, but—

PANTALONE: More to the point, did you see that?

TRUFFALDINO: The play?

PANTALONE: She is a woman!

TRUFFALDINO: She is indeed, sir, yes.

PANTALONE: Federigo Rasponi is a woman.

TRUFFALDINO: Yes, sir, we've established that, don't want to bore the audience. In that other play the women wore dresses and the men wore—

PANTALONE: Amazing!

TRUFFALDINO: Yes, sir. Now, if I can get back to my work—

PANTALONE: I am astonished! Overwhelmed! Bowled over! Why the hell aren't you?

TRUFFALDINO: Well, I had my suspicions, sir, and besides, I can't afford to be bowled over, I've got my chores to finish.

PANTALONE: Wait till Clarice hears this!

TRUFFALDINO: *(pushing one trunk to one side)* Man or woman, he—I mean, she—still needs my services. I'm sorry they're both so upset *(pushing other trunk aside)*, but life goes on, yes? Work's never done. And whatever happens, I don't want to risk another thrashing!

Scene 2

Lombardi and Pantalone cross toward each other from opposite directions.

LOMBARDI: Pantalone! Can't stand the man!

PANTALONE: Doctor Lombardi—your servant!

LOMBARDI: Of all the gall!

PANTALONE: Such a fortunate coincidence—I was about to pay you a visit.

LOMBARDI: To crow about the marriage, I suppose?

PANTALONE: No, no, no—we're back to square one.

LOMBARDI: Whatever that means.

PANTALONE: Quadrato uno! Quadrato uno!

LOMBARDI: I'm not an idiot.

PANTALONE: Uh . . . yes—right!

LOMBARDI: Stop shouting!

PANTALONE: If you'll let me explain—

111

LOMBARDI: Make it quick, I've got problems to solve, speeches to give, and—

PANTALONE: *(magnanimously)* My daughter shall marry your son forthwith.

LOMBARDI: Whom your daughter will marry no longer concerns me, or my son, or my illustrious and much wronged family. She may marry the Turin gentleman—or his servant!—for all we care. We don't give one jot or tittle—

PANTALONE: If you knew who the Turin gentleman was—

LOMBARDI: Couldn't care less! Your daughter has been seen with him, et hoc sufficit. We do not dabble in damaged goods. We do not haggle over unclaimed freight!

PANTALONE: I'll overlook that insult, but let me get a word in.

LOMBARDI: Too late for words after the deed is done!

PANTALONE: Nonsense! She is as intact as on the day she was born!

LOMBARDI: Do I make myself clear? It's no matter to me, or my progeny! We have done with you and your—family! *(leaves)*

PANTALONE: Of all the stuffed shirts I've ever—

SILVIO: *(entering)* Ah! The cause of my suffering!

PANTALONE: Signor Silvio! Suffer no longer!

SILVIO: *(drawing his sword)* You will not end my life, sir, until I've defended it to the death! *(to audience)* What?

PANTALONE: Please, please, enough swordplay for one day. I have something to tell you, and I'll make it quick, with no pauses, so you cannot interrupt me as some people do. This Signor Federigo business turns out to be a trick. My daughter has never wavered in her love for you—although she was ready to be dutiful to her father, I must say, as any good daughter should be—

SILVIO: Hurry up, hurry up!

PANTALONE: So if you still want her, you can have her.

SILVIO: Divine news!

PANTALONE: Well, I'm glad you've got your own opinion.

SILVIO: But how can I marry her when she's been the bride of another?

PANTALONE: *(to audience)* I spoke too soon. Papa's mouthpiece. *(to Silvio)* She hasn't. Because Federigo is really his sister, Beatrice.

SILVIO: An impostor!

PANTALONE: You got it.

SILVIO: But how did—

PANTALONE: I'll tell the story once, to you and Clarice at the same time.

SILVIO: I must apologize, sir. I went a little overboard in my passionate denun—

PANTALONE: Never mind, I understand. Incredible as it may seem, I've been in love many times myself. Think nothing of it. Now, come along!

SILVIO: *(leaving with Pantalone)* I am beside myself! Brotherhood is powerful!

Scene 3

Florindo enters, about to fall upon his dagger, restrained by Pandora. Beatrice ditto, restrained by Brighella.

BRIGHELLA: Over my dead body!

PANDORA: You're mad, sir, please!

BEATRICE: Let me go! *(breaking away)*

FLORINDO: Mind your own business! *(breaking away)*

BEATRICE: *(seeing him)* Have I lost my mind?

FLORINDO: *(seeing her)* Am I indeed mad?

BEATRICE: Florindo!

FLORINDO: Beatrice!

BEATRICE: Alive!

FLORINDO: You too!

BEATRICE: Fate!

FLORINDO: Destiny!

(they drop their weapons and embrace)

BRIGHELLA: Well, I'm glad that's settled—I was about to blow the whistle myself!

PANDORA: And think of the mess we don't have to clean up! *(leaves)*

BRIGHELLA: *(picking up daggers)* Just to be sure . . .

TRUFFALDINO: *(appearing at a window, seeing Beatrice and Florindo)* Uh-oh. *(observing without being seen)*

FLORINDO: I thought you were dead!

BEATRICE: And I, you! My servant—

FLORINDO: Mine too!

BEATRICE: This book—

FLORINDO: This portrait—

BEATRICE: Both in the same inn!

FLORINDO: Fate! And Federigo?

BEATRICE: Dead. No longer an obstacle to our happiness.

FLORINDO: Our servants deserve to be beaten.

BEATRICE: But we don't have the heart, given our happiness.

TRUFFALDINO: Glad to hear it.

BEATRICE: Yes, well! All this angst has left me a little frayed. I think I'll just freshen up. *(going into her room)*

FLORINDO: How I long to see her in women's clothes.

TRUFFALDINO: Now or never. Sir!

FLORINDO: Truffaldino! Tell me the truth about this portrait and your dead master!

TRUFFALDINO: You may have already guessed, sir—it's Pasqual's fault—that lady's servant. He mixed up everything, then begged me to shoulder the blame, since he was afraid she'd fire him. I'm a softie where Pasqual's concerned, so I shielded him, never dreaming that was your portrait, or that you'd take the death of the owner so hard. And that's the honest truth!

FLORINDO: The man you fetched the letter for was Signorina Beatrice's servant?

TRUFFALDINO: Yes, sir. Pasqual'.

FLORINDO: Why didn't you tell me that?

TRUFFALDINO: He begged me not to.

FLORINDO: What happened to loyalty?

TRUFFALDINO: Superseded by love of Pasqual'.

FLORINDO: The two of you deserve a beating.

TRUFFALDINO: The arithmetic's never on my side. Oh, sir—do you have the heart, given your happiness?

FLORINDO: Not really. Oh. Beatrice!

BEATRICE: *(offstage)* Dearest Florindo!

TRUFFALDINO: May I ask a favor, sir?

FLORINDO: What's that?

TRUFFALDINO: Well, you're not the only one in love. I'm in love with Signor Pantalone's maidservant, and if you could put in a word for me . . .

FLORINDO: Does the girl want you?

TRUFFALDINO: Does she want me? Does she want me? Oh, sir! Does she want me!

FLORINDO: You're overdoing it. Can you support her?

TRUFFALDINO: Well, she has a job, too. So we'd have a dual career marriage. And Pasqual' owes me.

FLORINDO: I wouldn't count on such a booby as this Pasqual'.

TRUFFALDINO: Sir, please—he's my dearest friend. I hate to hear a word against him. I love him like a brother. Nay, like a version of myself.

FLORINDO: Whatever you want. Now that I've found Beatrice, I'd do anything for anybody. *(goes into his room)*

TRUFFALDINO: Yes, sir! *(to audience)* I hope he means that. *(disappears, closing the window)*

(Clarice, her face veiled or otherwise concealed, staggers in, helped by Smeraldina, with Pantalone, Silvio, and Lombardi anxiously following)

PANTALONE: Daughter! You are overdoing this! If I've forgiven Silvio, you should, too!

(Clarice sighs extensively)

SILVIO: I wasn't myself, I didn't know what I was saying, I was so overwrought with the thought that I'd be left with naught, forever caught in—

LOMBARDI: Vengeance is mine, saith the Lord. Signorina, have pity, have mercy!

SMERALDINA: Look at it this way, Mistress. Men mistreat us one way or the other. So this one mistreated you once, what of it? You've got to marry somebody, why not him?

SILVIO: Well, thanks a lot, Smeraldina.

SMERALDINA: Don't mention it.

PANTALONE: *(to Lombardi)* Don't you have some mood-altering pills?

LOMBARDI: I don't do healing arts any more, I've got my hands full with the law. Look here, Signorina, we could sue you.

SILVIO: I don't think that's a good way to go, Father. Dearest Clarice, please say something! Punish me, call me every name in the book, but say something! Here I am—abject! At your feet! Have pity! One word—only one!

CLARICE: Rat!

PANTALONE: What? She said something!

LOMBARDI: *(to Silvio)* Strike while the iron is hot, boy, go to, go to!

SILVIO: If I thought my flowing blood would satisfy you, I would bleed before you. Instead of blood, take these tears as a sign of my infinite regret!

PANTALONE: Bravo!

LOMBARDI: Well said!

CLARICE: Rat!

PANTALONE: *(pulling Silvio to his feet)* Come along. *(to Clarice)* You too.

SMERALDINA: Didn't we do this before?

LOMBARDI: Join hands.

SILVIO: Signorina Clarice, for pity's sake—

CLARICE: Cruel!

SILVIO: Darling!

CLARICE: Nasty!

SILVIO: Angel!

CLARICE: Vile!

SILVIO: Beloved!

CLARICE: Ah!

PANTALONE: Going . . .

LOMBARDI: Going . . .

SILVIO: Forgive me.

CLARICE: I forgive you. *(they embrace)*

PANTALONE & LOMBARDI: Gone! *(they embrace)*

BRIGHELLA: *(entering)* Uh—excuse me, sirs.

PANTALONE: Brighella! Who assured me she knew Signor Federigo! Hah!

BRIGHELLA: Well, sir, I did my best. Wasn't everyone flummoxed? Almost identical twins, if you ask me.

PANTALONE: I did. And you turn out not to have known what you were talking about!

BRIGHELLA: I'd kiss it off, Signor, put it behind me— what's the point? Pazienza.

BEATRICE: *(entering)* Ladies and gentlemen, your pardon. I've caused some discomfort in your lives—please, forgive me.

CLARICE: Thank God you have found such deserved happiness! *(embracing her)*

SILVIO: Hey, hey, hey—

BEATRICE: You've got nothing to worry about.

LOMBARDI: An excess of spirit—have you tried leeches?

BEATRICE: What I did, I did for love.

PANTALONE: And you have found him at last?

SILVIO: Will you get married? Let's all get married together!

SMERALDINA: Count me in, sir.

SILVIO: No! Smeraldina?

SMERALDINA: Is that so preposterous? To the first man who walks through that arch.

PANTALONE: Ha-hah! *(walks through the arch)*

SMERALDINA: Uh—that would be a conflict of interest, sir, and redundant besides, since I'm already your servant.

PANTALONE: So? You're fired!

SMERALDINA: If you don't mind, and I'm sure you'll understand, such an understanding person as you yourself are and are known to be, trumpeted throughout all of Ven—

TRUFFALDINO: *(entering through the arch)* Your servant, signore e signorine!

SMERALDINA: I do not believe it, I do not! Signorina Clarice. *(rushing over)*

BEATRICE: Truffaldino! What's the story on this book, and your dead master?

TRUFFALDINO: Uh—Pasqual'. You may have heard of him. Always screwing up. He's really hopeless when it comes to getting the facts straight, or doing any of the ordinary things we servants do. He thought his master would send him away because he messed up really badly yet again, so I invented the story about his master's drowning, and I've been telling Signor Florindo that it was all my fault. For love of Pasqual'. And please—do not mention his name to the gentleman, or the jig will be up. For Pasqual'.

SMERALDINA: If you would recommend me to his mistress, please—so that she would allow him to marry me—oh, I'd be eternally grateful!

CLARICE: Whatever. Now that I'm reconciled with Silvio, I'd do anything.

(Florindo enters)

PANTALONE: Signor Florindo—congratulations on your good fortune!

LOMBARDI: Ditto, ditto.

PANTALONE: There is the little matter of unsettled accounts, but no matter, no matter, it will all turn out *(aside)* to my advantage.

LOMBARDI: Everything settled! Amor vincit omnia!

FLORINDO: One favor, Signor Pantalone.

PANTALONE: Your wish, my command.

FLORINDO: My servant wishes to marry your maid, Smeraldina. May he have your consent?

SMERALDINA: *(to audience)* Another suitor! Who could he be?

PANTALONE: Fine with me.

CLARICE: Signor Florindo! Oh! I promised to ask Father's consent for her to marry Beatrice's servant. Since you've spoken first . . . oh!

FLORINDO: Please, it's all right, I'll withdraw my request.

CLARICE: No, no, please.

FLORINDO: I insist. Not only do I withdraw. I unequivocally oppose such a match!

CLARICE: If she can't marry your man, she can't marry hers!

TRUFFALDINO: *(to audience)* You see what I mean about the arithmetic? Zip, zero.

SMERALDINA: They carry politeness too far!

PANTALONE: Aren't you being a bit . . . silly?

CLARICE: Gracious.

FLORINDO: Honorable.

SMERALDINA: Upper-class twits, if you ask me.

TRUFFALDINO: Please, I think I can settle this. Signor Florindo, didn't you ask that Smeraldina marry your servant?

FLORINDO: I did.

TRUFFALDINO: And Signorina Clarice, didn't you ask that Smeraldina marry Signorina Beatrice's servant?

CLARICE: As I'd promised.

TRUFFALDINO: Then give me your hand, Smeraldina.

PANTALONE: What right have you?

TRUFFALDINO: I am both servants.

FLORINDO: What?

BEATRICE: What?

TRUFFALDINO: *(to Florindo and Clarice)* Didn't you mean me?

FLORINDO & CLARICE: I did.

TRUFFALDINO: Ergo.

BEATRICE: *(to Florindo)* Isn't your servant called Pasqual'?

FLORINDO: I thought yours was called Pasqual'!

TRUFFALDINO: Please, please! I have given myself away—for love! I made a few snafus, but everything came out okay in the end, didn't it? So let's not quibble over minutiae, and get this show on the road.

(multiple nuptials and frivolity)